# ABOUT THE AUTHOR

Max Scratchmann was born in India in 1956. Brought "home" to Scotland as a small child he hated the cold climate and surgical grey light, and couldn't wait to get back to India again.

After university Max tried his hand at numerous jobs from dealing in antiques to selling outsized ladies' underwear and eventually became a full time freelance illustrator and writer in 1984.

He is the author of the acclaimed autobiography, **The Last Burrah Sahibs**, about his childhood in Bengal, and his book about downshifting in the Scottish Islands, **Chucking It All**, was named one of the ten best travel books of 2009 by Worldhum.

Max now lives and works in Edinburgh, a city said to be rivalled only by Venice for culture and architecture in the entirety of western Europe, where, amongst other things, he is a popular performance poet.

He is the author of three travel books, two books of verse and many short stories.

**By the Same Author**

The Last Burrah Sahibs
Chucking It All
Bad Girls
My Rubber Hebrew Nose
Bodice Rippers & Carnie Strippers

# Scotland for Beginners

## Learning to Live in the Land of My Fathers

### Max Scratchmann

First Edition 2013

Published in the UK, USA & Europe by
Poison Pixie Publishing

www.poisonpixie.com

All rights reserved. No part of this publication may be reproduced, stored in a retrieval system or recorded by any means without prior written permission from the publisher.

The right of Max Scratchmann to be identified as the author of this work has been asserted by him in accordance with the Copyright, Designs and Patents Act 1988.

© Copyright Max Scratchmann 2013

**ISBN 978-0-9571920-5-8**

A CIP record for this book is available from the British Library.

This book may not, in whole or in part, be resold, distributed, shared physically or electronically, posted on internet sites or journals; nor may any of the characters, scenarios and locations contained herein be featured in fictions, 'fan fictions' or scenarios.

This book is provided subject to the condition that it shall not, by way of trade or otherwise, be lent, re-sold, hired out, or otherwise circulated without the publisher's prior consent in any form of binding or cover other than that in which it is published and without a similar condition including this condition being imposed on the subsequent purchaser.

**ACKNOWLEDGMENTS**

A longer version of "Bingo!" originally appeared in Chapman magazine

# CHRONOLOGY

Max Scratchmann was born in Calcutta, India, in 1956 and was first brought to Dundee in Scotland as a small baby, but he doesn't remember that. At that time his family of four stayed in his dad's aunty's house, all of them squeezing into one room for the duration of their four-month stay.

In the bitter winter of 1963 the family returned to Scotland, having bought a house there at the conclusion of their last visit, and Max was suddenly thrown into a world quite alien to anything he had previously known.

His father returned to India alone that year, leaving a barely seven-years-old Max with his mother and teenage sister behind to cope with their new lifestyle until he 'retired' from the East in 1966.

However in 1967, when it looked as though the colonial lifestyle of the Scottish Jute Wallahs was finally over, a three-year job-offer for East Pakistan (now Bangladesh) arrived in the post and, jumping at it, the entire family headed out East once again, finally returning to Scotland in the summer of 1970.

*Our House, Barnagore Jute Factory, Calcutta*

# PROLOGUE

## CALCUTTA, INDIA
## NOVEMBER 1962

*With my sister on the promenade, Barnagore Jute Factory*

## 1 - Home Leave

The winter sun burns white in the cloudless sky while laden jute barges chug contentedly down the Hooghly river, their jaunty captains calling out ribald greetings to each other across the turbulent water. At the jetty a brightly painted steamer, bound for up-river, has stopped to pick up passengers, and its ready-to-sail hooter sounds sharply amidst a flutter of multi-coloured parrots which whirl noisily up into the sky.

I, meanwhile, am furiously pedalling my bike along the immaculately swept promenade - a perfect replica of the south embankment of the Thames - my ayah swishing sedately along behind me in a sparkling azure-blue sari, calling out periodic words of caution about my speed that I, of course, completely ignore.

It's just a little before noon, but even in November the mid-morning sun is reaching the end of its tolerable period, and I wipe a thin film of sweat from my brow. "Come on, Madeline," I cry, turning my callipered cycle up the long flower-bed-edged drive that leads to our river-front mansion house, "let's go back inside, it's getting hot and I need a Coca Cola."

"Oh, maybe now is not a good time, Chotta Sahib," my ayah calls portentously to my retreating back, "for your amah is very busy this morning and not in the best of moods..." But I have already cycled on up the drive and am running up the long flight of whitewashed concrete steps to the house.

*

I speed quickly through the shady veranda where our mynah bird calls out a cheeky greeting to me, perfectly impersonating my dad's voice, then burst into the lounge on route to the dining room pantry with its huge pre-war fridge and endless supply of soft drinks; but come abruptly to a halt at the scene that greets me. Instead of the normal oasis of calm in an otherwise bustling household, our usually tranquil living room is alive with people and boxes, and swathe after swathe of very unfamiliar clothing is being packed into large sea chests which lie open in a semi circle like the coffins of Dracula's brides.

"I thought I told you to keep him outside," my mother snaps at my perspiring ayah who has run up, puffing, behind me. "There's a hundred bally things still to do and I can't have the blighter under my damn feet. *No, not that one, that one.* I told you, overcoats go in the chests, we only need one set of warm clothes in the cabin trunks. Honestly, why we have to go parading off to that damn country in the winter I do not know. Madeline, take Max to the play room before I have heart failure. No, Ali, not that one, *that* one!"

*

Sitting in my room looking out over the flat top roof of the floor below, a line of Madeline's brightly coloured washing flapping discreetly in the bright noon-day sun, I truculently sip my Coke and play at out-staring my dear old ayah until she finally relents and tells me what's going on.

"The Manager Sahib is due for leave, and you are all to return home next week," she tells me, stroking my hair. "You will be going to Bombay by train to board a great ocean liner and then crossing the seas to the famous city of Dundee in the England, near her majesty the Queen."

"The England?" I say, quizzically.

"Belite," she translates, using the Bengali word for Britain and I nod sagely, comprehending.

"And what will we do once we are there, Madeline, and why are you not coming too?"

Madeline laughs. "Ah," she sighs, "I am indeed a Christian Bengali, but I fear that you would not want to be seen with me in such an illustrious place, where you will become a very fine gentleman indeed and will not have time for an old Hindi woman such as I…"

"No, no," I say vehemently, hugging her, "I don't want to go to the Belite if you can't come too!"

She smiles benignly, disentangling my octopus arms and going over to the high bookshelf where I am not permitted to play. "Here,

here are the photographs that the Manager Sahib took the last time that you were in Belite. See, that is you, a tiny *baccha* in your dear amah's arms, and, see, there, there is the Manager Sahib's fine house just a few minutes away from the palace of her majesty, Queen Elizabeth."

I slacken my grip on her waist long enough to peer cautiously at the little monochrome rectangles on the matt black page of the album, each carefully annotated in white paint in my father's neat hand. "It's a bit small, isn't it," I say, frowning, surveying the snapshots of a neat grey bungalow beneath a lowering Scottish sky…

# PART ONE

## DUNDEE, SCOTLAND
## 1963 – 67

*Putting our old Belfast sink to good use*

## 2 - Taking Tea with the Aunties

It's what passes for a fine spring day in the Dundee of 1963 and my friend, George Brice, and I are huddled round the tiny circle of warmth the gas fire affords, playing with Lego. My parents have been talking heatedly in the kitchen, my mother banging pots truculently at the sink, but eventually a consensus is reached and my father strides through to the living room and tells me to get my coat, we're going out for afternoon tea.

"Can George come too?" I ask innocently and my father nods. "The more the merrier," my mother mutters dryly.

Fresh from India and the sophistication of Calcutta émigré society, my idea of afternoon tea usually involves decamping to the cool shade of Firpo's or Trinka's restaurants, their acres of starched white table cloths and mouth-watering patisserie making them the European watering holes of choice. And, though I know that there is nothing quite like this here, George has told me at length about his family's Saturday trips to the Café Val D'Or - a bustling eatery which boasts of a trendy fruit squash machine with plastic oranges swirling around in a glazed in spin-dryer of coloured liquid - and my pal and I spend the entire bus journey from our glacial white-harled estate to the towering tenements of the town centre planning an inaugural repast of cheese rolls followed by Macaroon Bars and red Bona Cola.

However, all our gastronomical dreams turn to ashes as we

behold, waiting for us to alight from the green and cream open-backed omnibus, three stern fur-clad ladies like bedraggled beady-eyed rooks, and I realise with a sinking feeling that this is not going to be tea, but Tea with the Aunties.

"Just what have you got me into?" George asks under his breath as we are chastely embraced by the old ladies and breathe in their musty aroma of aged fabrics and subdued perfume.

"I'm so sorry," I whisper back behind my handkerchief, "I thought we were just having our tea."

"Welcome to my world," my mother says, almost imperceptibly, from behind us.

*

It appears that the only suitable establishments for ladies of the stature of my father's unholy triumvirate of female relatives to take high tea are the restaurants of the two competing department stores that stand facing each other at the head of Commercial Street in the city centre. The Aunties' favourite, D M Brown's, stands sedately on the left, while, on the right its deadly rival, G L Wilson's[1] glowers menacingly across the busy thoroughfare as we enter the revolving door of the ladies' favoured retailer.

---

[1] Readers of The Broons will know these establishments as G L Brown's and D M Wilson's – Dundee's little in-joke on the rest of Scotland.

The Beatles have already released *Please Please Me* while *She Loves You* stands waiting in the wings, yet as we walk into D M Brown's staid Panopticum that day it is as if time has stood still in 1938 and hasn't moved much since. Additionally, unlike the bustling Co-op mothership in nearby Peter Street, D M Brown's is not a child-friendly emporium, and a stern commissionaire at the door ensures no unattended juveniles ever enter these hallowed halls, and black-frocked assistants keep a weather eye on anyone under five-foot lest we stray momentarily from the parental leash and wreck havoc amongst the dusty bolts of fabric.

The aunties, however, are welcomed with open arms and they lead the way through the plushly carpeted isles like ships in full sail, entering the rickety lift with its brass fittings and uniformed attendant like the royal party boarding the Britannia.

George and I have been reverently hushed up until now, not because we have, overnight, realised our rightful places as minors and sworn a vow of silence, but because the store with its acres of wood-panelling and brass has captivated us, but now, within the confines of the elevator, irrepressible mischief begins to take hold.

In the name of "smartening us up" my dad has brilliantined our hair down after giving it a scalp-tingling brushing, slapping on a locally produced pomade that feels like an unholy alliance of wallpaper paste and shellac, and the aforementioned goo instantly sets hard on our tousled heads, turning our unruly locks into brittle mats that sit on our craniums like petrified doormats.  Now, however, having withstood the sharp April breeze and the rough and tumble of the bus journey to town, our tamed tresses begin to rebel in the slightly claustrophobic heat of the brass and mahogany lift, and first George's and then my hair begins to ping upwards in rebellious spikes and strands.

I look at George and he looks at me, as twig-like strands of hair begin to go here, there and everywhere, and a giggle begins to bubble up inside me.  My mother catches my eye and glares warningly at me, but it is already too late, and within seconds my friend and I are helpless with laughter, much to the chagrin of the Aunties who hiss, "Wheesht, laddies!  We're in the lift" simultaneously at us.

"Third floor. Bedding, electrical and tea lounge," the elevator man smoothly interrupts in a soft rounded voice, holding the doors open for the Aunties to alight, "have a nice afternoon, ladies, thank you.  The chef says the haddock's particularly fine the day."

The Aunties nod graciously for the culinary tip, unsure just how friendly one ought to be with the lift mannie, and head out toward the cafe, distancing themselves from George and myself, their ratty fox fur collars bouncing behind them, three pairs of glassy dead-rodent eyes watching our every move.

"Told you they all had eyes in the backs of their heads, didn't I," my mother whispers in my ear, "they can see everything you do!"

"Wheesht, Lassie, we're in the store," the Aunties hiss, rounding on her as one.

*

The meal passes relatively uneventfully. Disregarding our requests for cheese rolls, the Aunties have decided that everyone should have the famed haddock and order it for the table, along with a pot of tea and two concessionary orange squashes for myself and George. A stony-faced waitress who looks about a hundred and ten years old takes our order wordlessly, but looks at me sharply when orange squash is mentioned.

"We don't have any straws," she says slowly and without humour, her piggy eyes boring into me, "we find that small boys misbehave themselves grievously when given straws."

I'm about to make some reply to this when my father quickly cuts in. "Just in the glass will be fine, thanks, and I'll keep my eye on the boys' tumblers."

"Aye, weel," the waitress says dubiously, shutting her little pad with a resounding snap. "It'll be a wee whilie for your haddock, someone's been telling all the folks to order it and the chef's up at ninety-nine."

*

Eventually the table is cleared and a second silver teapot – tastefully engraved "D M Brown's" – is set down, along with a tall three-tier cake stand. The Aunties, who have so far only clucked about the excellence of the fish, now rub their hands in delight, and allocate baked confectionery to everyone according to their deserveability.

"Chic, you'll be wanting a fruit slice. They're no' quite as good as my own, but there's always a good quality of currant in these ones. Not like all yon strange fruit you'll have been eating in India, I'm sure. I don't know if it's healthy, you know, eating the same food as all those darkies. Rosie, are you having cake or are you watching your waistline? You are, oh well, one more won't kill you, eh?"

My mother scowls and says nothing, but takes the proffered scone – "It's plain, you know, not fattening" – and ostentatiously spreads a thick layer of butter on it then tops it with jam, while the Three Witches shake their heads and carry on with their distribution.

Oblivious of their own waistlines the Aunties now all help themselves to Nicoll & Smibert's meringues, but George and I are only entrusted with a chocolate biscuit each lest we make a mess on the restaurant's starched white tablecloth with unsightly crumbs, and our request for a second glass of orange squash is strenuously denied on the grounds that we're getting the bus home and that we'll embarrass everyone by needing to visit the [very low voice] *toilet* on the return journey.

Eventually, though, all that is going to be consumed is eaten and the grumpy waitress begins to count the remaining cakes before laying the bill face down at my father's side. However, there are several wrapped biscuits remaining, and, before she completes her tally, she makes a great show of methodically prodding each one with a stubby little finger, glaring at George and me while she does so.

"We find that small boys like to play jokes with the biscuits and think that they are very clever, but we are older and wiser here and know all the tricks that young minds can think up," she tells us in all seriousness, "so don't be thinking that you can play tricks and get free biscuits in *this* restaurant."

"You hear what she says," the Aunties hiss like a Greek chorus of complicit Mrs Joe Gargeries, "don't *ever* play jokes with the biscuits."

I nod, hoping against hope that the waitress will stab the remaining Tunnock's Tea Cake with equal force, but it is, sadly, not to be and the cake total is tallied up and the bill calculated. However, as a fitting postscript, I hear my mother bending my father's ear that night after I have been put to bed, her aggrieved voice declaiming, "…and you let that bally waitress accuse Max of stealing her stupid damn biscuits…"

I drift off to a deep and welcome sleep, feeling well and truly vindicated...

## 3 - The Baths

Life, for British children in India, always revolves around sunny days at the mill swimming pool, so when my sister asks me if I fancy a dip one Saturday morning, I readily agree.

Thus we duly arrive at the faded but rather grand Victorian edifice of the Dundee Public Baths, a somewhat gothic structure that sits staidly on the river front, and gingerly enter its boomy interior. Inside it's like stepping into a decayed Arabian palace rather than the breezy open air swimming pools that we are used to, but though the foyer is ornately tiled it smells strongly of carbolic and chlorine, and there's a queue of unruly small boys at the ticket office awaiting admission.

Used to being the mill manager's children and just walking straight into the pool when we want to swim, it seems odd to have to wait in line here, but we stand patiently and eventually reach the ticket window where we come face to face with an officious woman in a bright pink nylon overall who glares at us suspiciously.

"Two please," my sister says, slightly disconcerted by the attendant's Medusa stare, but the woman continues to glower at us.

"Just the two dips then, is it?" she queries. "You've got your own costumes, and towels and soap, have you?"

My sister nods.

"And what about verrucas?  Do you either of you have any verrucas?"

We have no idea what verrucas are, but hastily deny all knowledge of possessing them, and the woman grunts.  "Alright, that's two shillings, then.  Are you going to mixed bathing or do you want to go to the ladies' pool, Lass?  Both to mixed, alright, here's your tickets, straight through the turnstile and to your left."

My sister lays her money down and two pieces of buff-coloured paper judder out from the engraved brass ticket counter like a stuttering tapeworm and we step gingerly through the turnstile and look around us for the water.  There are some lopsided signs saying "Turkish Bath" and "Ladies' Bathing" but, as promised, to the left there is, indeed, a swaying double door under the letters, "Mixed Bathing Pond".

I'm suddenly reticent to proceed, but my sister is just about to turn seventeen and wants to prove that she's ready to take on the world, so she pushes open the swing doors like John Wayne entering a saloon and we stride into the wave of steamy heat that engulfs us.

*

The pool is seething with humanity and the noise under its cracked frosted glass ceiling is louder than Bedlam. There are two rows of old wooden changing cubicles on the left and right, their rickety doors warped from over a century's exposure to the water, and a rather shaky-looking diving board wobbles precariously at the far end of the pond.

"Tickets!" a voice yells, and we turn to see a counter like a prison's inmates' processing office where a florid-faced fat man with a whistle round his neck stands before row upon row of ingenious metal-framed half-body hangers that hold people's clothing and shoes in the one contraption.

"Tickets, Lass," he says again, this time with growing impatience in his voice, and my sister quickly hands over our vouchers and is presented with two empty versions of the aforementioned clothing cages that, naked, as it were, look a bit like sinister robot skeletons. "You change on the left, Lass, but the wee lad needs to use the men's side. You've twenty minutes, best get a move on."

*

The wire-frame hanger is almost as big as I am and feels like hefting a stripped-down tailor's dummy along the slippery wet poolside, but I lug it manfully along the row of changing rooms, trying not to look at the vaguely comic vignettes of wet feet and knobbly knees under the half doors as I go, and eventually find an empty cubicle and change. I've no fear of water, and, as soon I've deposited my clothes with the corpulent attendant, I dive headlong into the first clear stretch of water that I see.

*Grooch!!* I surface spluttering like a dog who's bitten on a lemon as I spit lungfuls of cold and very salty water out of my mouth. What *is* this stuff, brine? I look around me for my sister, but, before I can spot her, I'm deafened by a piercing whistle and turn to see a clone of the blustery-faced clothing attendant standing on the poolside waving his hands violently in my direction.

"Get oot, get oot," he yells, "you've just dived straight in!"

"It's a pool, isn't it?" I say, perplexed, treading water, "that's what I normally do…"

The man slaps his fat fist to his beefy forehead and groans. "In the name o' the wee man, where've you come from, son? You cannae go jumping into the pool just like that. You need to shower first."

"Oh," I say, "there are showers?"

The man clasps his head again, but before further dialogue can ensue my sister appears and takes charge, and I am marched up to the far end of the pool where I am cleansed of all possible infection and we finally go into the water and start to swim.

Once you get used to it, the cool salt water which feeds in straight from the river mouth outside is buoyant and supportive, and together we swim length after length, dodging the many bodies that fill the greyish water like victims of the sunk Titanic, until my limbs start to get tired and we clamber out at the deep end, showering down again before we go back to the front desk to collect our clothes and towels.

The first fat man is taking someone else's ticket, so we stand waiting our turn, cold now and our legs goose pimpled, until he finally turns to us.

"Oh, it's you pair, *finally*," he says swearing softy under his breath, "are you quite finished now, are you? Twenty minutes, I said to you. Twenty minutes. No' two bloody hours. Did you no' hear me whistling on you? Were you no' watching the time?"

"You've got our watches…" I start to say but my sister shushes me.

"I'm awfully sorry," she says making her eyes as big as Bambi's, "we've not been here before and we didn't hear your whistle amongst all the other whistles that were going off."

"And there *were* lots," I add.

The fat man grunts and looks slightly mollified. "There are your clothes," he says stiffly, indicating an ungainly heap on the damp ground, "dinnae trespass on my good nature like this the next time you come."

*Me demonstrating the latest thing in shorts-suits*

## 4 - Chinese Food

The most popular Chinese restaurant in Calcutta is a palatial establishment known as the Waldorf, a cool roomy eatery with frescos of China on the walls and huge dye-cut dragons with glowing eyes guarding its inner portico. On a typical Sunday night in the early sixties, however, although there may be a smattering of Indian faces at its white-clothed tables, the eating place is populated by leathery old Dundonian mill hounds, and the hubbub of conversation is peppered with multiple references to the chances of Dundee over United in the Scottish cup.

Given this dedication to the cuisine of the orient, then, you would expect the Bamboo Café, the first Chinese bistro to grace the grey sandstone streets of Dundee, to be mobbed with eager epicures anxious to sample its delights, but, when my family first announce our intention of dining there the reaction of our neighbours is less than favourable.

"Are you actually going to *eat* in there?" Cissy from next door says with palpable horror in her voice. "How can you be sure that they won't touch your food with their hands?"

"And what about the menu?" Jean from two along chimes in, "is it not all in those Chinese character things? How will you read it?"

My dad laughs. "It's only rice and noodles," he says with a grin, "it doesn't bite."

"Ah, but is it not all in a sauce?" Cissy insists, "you've no idea what they could be putting in there when it's all covered up like that. Oh, it's all right for you folk, what with eating curried snakes' eyes and things in India and all that, you're used to it, but I think I'd end up with a gyppy tummy if I ever went to a weird place like yon."

My dad laughs again and pulls me to him. "Well, this one's grown up on it and it hasn't done him any harm."

"Well, not yet…" Jean from two along says portentously.

*

Unlike the Calcutta Waldorf, the Bamboo Café is not a place of wonderment for a small boy – it later became a Wimpy bar – with its plain magnolia walls and crowded-in tables. However, we're hit by the familiar Chinese restaurant scent of sesame oil and five spice powder as we enter, and the aroma alone is sufficient to transport me back to the more exotic world I have previously inhabited before our enforced homecoming.

Dundee in the early sixties boasts of very little in the way of food choices, and main meals consist largely of minced or stewed beef, with perhaps the added thrill of a steak pie on Sunday or Wallace's bridies after the weekly excursion to Woolworth's on a Saturday morning. Therefore, to my young mind, a people so starved of variety should be beating down the doors to sample something new, but the Bamboo Café's tables are mostly vacant, and of the two parties already present when we walk in, one is made up of ex-India acquaintances of my parents.

However, unlike the effusive welcoming from the staff of the Waldorf, our arrival is greeted with implacable indifference by the bored Chinese manager who stands by his idle cash register, his face a study in disillusionment with the promised riches of the West, and a gregarious young local woman in waitress garb herds us to the nearest vacant table.

"Come away ben and have a seat," she chirrups, throwing menu cards in our general direction, "and just give me a shout if you're no' sure what the food is and I'll translate!"

My mother shoots her a glance of withering disdain but my father makes some quip to keep the peace, and, starved of exotica these last two months, we eagerly grab the bills of fare and scan the columns for our favourite dishes.

"Oh look, they've got lychees," my sister gasps.

"Yes, at five shilling a damn portion," my mother interjects, "so don't you two be getting carried away."

"Oh, leave them be," my dad interrupts, "we're out for our dinner."

"Hark at Mister Bally-Bigshot-Moneybags, more money than

sense," my mother mutters dryly from behind her large laminated card, but further jovial family banter is halted by the return of the chirpy waitress.

"Hello, hello, have you made up your minds then?" she laughs, pencil poised, "or is it all a wee bitty strange to you?"

"No, we know what we want," my mother says icily.

"Oh, professionals like them at table one, eh," says the girl who has surely been a barmaid before this gig, since she bears no resemblance to the snooty ice-maiden-waitress who had served us in D M Brown's tea room when we'd visited with the Aunties a fortnight previously.

"I'll have prawn fried rice," my mother says, ignoring the mild jibe, "and a small portion of sweet and sour pork."

"And chow mein for me," my dad chimes in, "the special chicken one with the fried egg on top."

"And I'll have shrimp foo yung," interjects my recently-turned-seventeen-year-old sister, "but just boiled rice with that, I'm watching my weight!"

"Oh, hold on, hold on," says the girl, her pencil flying over her little pad, "mighty, you folks know your stuff, do you not? Now, anything to drink?"

"Hang on, you've not taken my order yet," I say, aggrieved, and the girl looks down at me in wonderment.

"My, the wee lad's wanting to order his own dinner. Jings, is he no' a bold one," the waitress says to the table in general, then turning to my mother, adds in a loud stage whisper, "is he *allowed* to do that?"

Since as far back as I can remember I have given my nightly dinner order to Squinty, our faithful bearer back in India, and have been choosing and ordering my own restaurant selections for almost as long, so I'm not sure what's upsetting this chippie, but my father, sensing an imminent cultural clash, quickly intervenes before my mother can weigh in.

"The boy's been brought up in India, it's what they do over there," he says by way of explanation, and the girl raises her eyebrows.

"India? My my, that's awfully far away, isn't it? Me, I've never been further than a trip across the Tay on the Fifie. We went all the way to St Andrew's once. Man, that was rare. Oh, sorry, Laddie, I've no' taken your order. What was it you were wanting, Lambie?"

*

The food arrives and, compared to what we've been eating these past few weeks, it is a banquet beyond compare, but my mother remains stubbornly unimpressed.

"They call this a prawn," she says disgustedly, spearing the unfortunate mollusc on the prongs of her fork before swallowing it whole, "why if our cook bought that at the bally bazaar as a shrimp I'd send him straight back with it."

The non-Indian contingent at the next table, who have ordered boiled ham and chips, by the way, look over in our direction, aghast, it being a complete social taboo in the Dundee of the era to utter *any* word of complaint in a restaurant, regardless if they've just served you up fried worms instead of trifle.

My father smiles kindly. "Ah, but we're not on the Hooghly anymore," he says, patting her hand placatingly, "and there's not so many prawns to be had in the Tay."

My mother opens her mouth to reply, but is silenced by the intervention of the party of Jute Wallahs from table one who are getting up to leave.

"Aye, it's no' the Waldorf, is it not, Rose," a florid-faced man booms, "but it's the only place we've got, so we take what we get and like it. Cheerio the now, folks, see you all next week! Oh, and the lychees are great, Max, but you'll no' get a bunch[2]!"

---

[2] In India, lychees are purchased from the fruit bazaar in bunches of a hundred, laboriously shelled by patient cooks and then served at table on ice.

"How many for five bally shillings?" my mother calls after them but the man only chuckles.

"It's a night out, Rosie, live a little!" he laughs as they vanish out of the door.

*With my sister*

## 5 - The Minister's Little Joke

It's a sunny afternoon in early May and I'm sitting playing with my building set while my dad paints the newly installed living room radiator, hunkered down below the window sill on his hands and knees.  After a while he pauses to straighten his back, and, to his great surprise, spies a darkly-clad man in an oversized black homburg standing by the front gate looking about him bewilderedly.  Their eyes meet for a brief second and then, not recognising the stranger, my father shrugs and gets back to his painting, vanishing below the sill again like an exiting puppet in a seaside Punch & Judy show.

"Who was that, Dad?" I ask and my father shakes his head.

"No idea, Chummo," he replies, "probably an encyclopaedia salesman looking for an easy mark."

I have no idea what either an encyclopaedia or an easy mark are, but Dad seems content with the explanation so I go back to my building blocks.  My father, likewise, gets back to his work and slaps paint happily for a minute or two, then straightens up to replenish his brush and comes face to face with the black-hatted stranger who's now peering down at him from directly outside the window.

"What the hell…" Dad exclaims and then sees the dog-collar. "Oh, sorry, Padre, I didn't realise, what can I do for you?"

The Minister laughs. "Well, if you're Chic, the man I'm looking for, you can start by making me a cup of tea. I've been doing my rounds all day and my feet are *killing* me. I'm your minister, by the way, Cissy from next door said that you were back from India so I thought I'd come over and meet you all. Though I think that you were maybe playing a wee game of hide and seek with me just now, were you not?" he says with a laugh, well amused at his own little joke.

## 6 - Miss Hannah Regrets...

Miss Hannah is the long-suffering lady who stands stalwartly behind the mahogany and glass counter of the Co-operative boys' wear department in the bowels of the building. A thin fidgety woman in her sixties, she favours dark navy, wears big horn-rim spectacles and opaque lisle stockings but dyes her long hair, which is always worn in a tight bun, a defiant flame red.

She is standing in her customary stork-like pose behind her counter in the gloomy basement when my mother and I walk in, a pale freckly-faced wraith of a woman with her brogues sitting neatly in the groove that forty years of waiting on small boys and their mothers has worn for her.

"Oh my, and is it not yourselves, then?" she says brightly but without any real warmth as we approach, "back from India again then, are we? I had another lady and her young men in here the other week, they'd been overseas too. Very tanned they all were, almost like darkies. Not that *you're* like that, of course, Madam, in fact, I've always meant to compliment you on your complexion. How do you keep your skin so white in all that heat? Oh gracious, listen to me, blethering on and on. You'll be wanting new school clothes for this young man, will you not? Yes, they grow so much at this age, do they not? I can see he's already pushing his elbows through the jumper we had sent out to you. We're getting to be Dundee's answer to William Whiteley's, are we not?"

My mother smiles guardedly. "Yes, he's big for his age, isn't he?" she says noncommittally.

"Oh my, yes *indeed*, Madam," Miss Hannah immediately coos with the same enthusiasm that she would have used to agree that I had been converted into a giraffe if my mother had declared it so. "A good few inches taller than any boy his age I've seen this last three months, yes, indeed."

My mother coughs politely.

"The boy needs…" she begins, but Miss Hannah intercedes.

"A complete new set of school clothes, Madam, of course, and we have it all in stock and in all the correct tonal shades too. Not a generic navy or anything like that. The real McCoy for his primary school. That's why we're the Dundee Sosh, of course, because we look after Dundee people and know exactly what they need. Now, let me just slip my tape measure round your waist, young man, yes, it's a just a little cold, isn't it, just like a doctor's stethoscope. That's it, say 'ah', oh my, I'm only joking, you don't really need to say 'ah' for me. Oh well, you go ahead and say it if you like. My but he's grown, it's all yon sunshine abroad, I suspect. So, it's new shorts and a school jumper, is it, and do you want a spare jumper for the school, Madam? No? No problem, just the one then. Max, take these shorts and away into the changing cubicle with you to try them one. Off you go now, you wee scamp, and will you want two white shirts or more, Madam, they're Bri-Nylon and drip dry, so you can wash one and wear one, and socks, five pairs with garters?"

"These feel a bit loose…" I say from behind the dusty velvet curtain of the dark changing room.

"Loose? Surely not," Miss Hannah cries, mortally offended, "why, you saw me measure him myself, Madam, how on earth can they be loose?"

The heavy cubicle curtain is unceremoniously wrenched to one side and Miss Hannah strides into the changing room with my mother in her wake.

"No, a lovely neat fit," she declares, thrusting her hand down the waistband of my shorts and tugging violently, "smart but casual and just right across the stomach."

"They're not *too* tight, are they?" asks my mother, likewise hauling at my trousers, "the fellow's still growing, you know. Have you left some room for that?"

"Oh, Madam, what a wee joke! If I had them any looser they'd be round his wee ankles, so they would. Of course, if you'd like them a bit looser that's no problem. We can always get them altered to fit braces on them, save the wee laddie any embarrassment, if you catch my drift."

"I think these fit fine…" I say to no-one in particular, completely regretting having ever spoken and praying that there is nobody else in the store to witness my humiliation.

"Oh my, now he says they fit, Madam," says Miss Hannah rather petulantly. "Do they fit, Madam, or is it to be the braces? We have a very attractive range of braces in all the tartans. Will I show them to you?"

"I don't know, I'm not very keen on him wearing braces…" my mother says, hesitating.

"Oh no, of course not," Miss Hannah agrees, chameleon-like, "they're more of an older man's thing, anyway, not really suitable for a boy of his age."

"The shorts really do fit," I say with more desperation than hope in my voice.

"Och, the wee lad's fair mortified, is he not," says the suddenly diplomatic Miss Hannah taking my mother by the arm, "come away ben, Madam, and I'll show you our range of school socks. Will you need garters too, or do you prefer to make those yourself?"

*

Eventually our purchases are neatly wrapped in brown paper and my mother's money is placed in a metal container and sent off down a brass tube to the cash office with a self-satisfied hiss.

"A pleasure, as always, Madam," Miss Hannah says with a frigid smile, noting my mother's share number in her neat ledger, "it's fine to see he's grown so tall since the last time you brought him in. We'll be seeing you both again soon, I hope? I do so look forward to your visits, you know. Well, cheerio the now, and don't you be strangers, Madam, there's always a welcome for you at the Sosh…"

As we turn to go Miss Hannah's right foot sneaks up to the back of her left calf and her eyes close down, as though her whole body falls into suspended animation until her next customer wakes her from her Sleeping Beauty's castle of idleness. She is still there the next time I need my sartorial requirements met, and the next, but when I celebrate my tenth birthday a brusque young man has taken her place.

"Miss Hannah? I never knew her. I think she retired last year," he says, barely stifling a yawn. "Now, what can I get you folks? School clothes, is it?"

And that seems to be the end of the story, but a few weeks later we're taking our books back to the library at Coleside when I see the legendary Miss H going into the Five Ways pensioner's club with some of her friends and call out a cheerful greeting.

The other ladies turn and nod but the still defiantly flame-haired Miss Hannah just keeps on going, oblivious.

It seems that after forty years of tirelessly meeting the public's needs Miss Hannah regrets she's unable to smile today…

## 7 - Bread and Butter Beatniks

Despite the main store's distinctly old-school mode of appearance, the record department of D M Brown's is *the* in-place to purchase music for my sister and her friends, and I consider myself highly privileged to be taken along for retail therapy there one sunny Saturday afternoon.

We have become regular listeners to Radio Luxembourg, who, my sister says, offer a far better selection from the current pop charts than the BBC Home Service, and we have fallen in love with a song called *Bread and Butter* and have decided to purchase it today.

We have pestered our mother unceasingly for the money for this until she finally capitulates, and, armed with a newly-acquired ten shilling note, we speed promptly down town to D M's music emporium, a sacred temple for teenage girls of the era, its interior lined with large posters of all the current heart-throbs from The Beatles to the photogenic young Peter Noone of Herman's Hermits. And there are girls *everywhere*. Love-sick girls in ankle socks and white Alice bands lounging languidly at the counters; bespectacled Beatnik student-types leafing furtively through the LP browsers; and even short-skirted Mods twisting mutely within the glass-fronted listening booths like eels glistening in waterless tanks.

"We'll need to push in here," my sister mutters as a sales girl in a black and white striped jumper and wearing more mascara than can possibly be good for her sticks her head over the counter like a cow peeping over a hedge.

"Hiya, you ains," she chirrups good naturedly, "what are you after the day?"

My sister waves our newly acquired ten bob note. "Bread and Butter," she says with a grin.

The assistant's face clouds under her makeup for a second. "Bread and butter? What are you talking about? Oh aye, I get it, that New Beats song that's been on Luxy all week. No, sorry, we're sold out."

We look at her horrified, seeking for some clue that might alert us to the fact that we're having our legs pulled and that the apparent lack of our chosen melody is nothing more than an elaborate hoax. But the assistant's countenance doesn't falter. "Honest to God," she says, spreading her palms outwards in a gesture of supplication, "we've no' got it. Try doon the road."

*

We work our way along the bustling Murraygate with its defunct tram lines and hoards of Saturday shoppers and eventually cross over to the seedier Wellgate and its maze of run-down shops and cafés. We try a couple of places here without success and finally come upon the last resort, a small store just off the beaten track whose unenthusiastic sign simply says, "Music".

"They'll not have it," I say pessimistically.

"Well, we'll ask anyway," my sister replies, pushing open the door.

*

There are no listening booths or pictures of the Beatles in this establishment, and Scottish accordion music jangles cheerily through hidden speakers behind yellow pegboard walls that are lined with faded EP covers of grey-haired men in kilts. I recognise Kenneth McKeller and Andy Stewart from television at the Aunties' house, but the rest of them could be tartan Martians for all their grinning faces mean to us.

However, the place appears to be as deserted as a Celtic Marie Celeste at first glance, but we suddenly spot the proprietor, a mousy little white-haired man in baggy trousers and a checked waistcoat which may have fitted around his bulging pot belly a decade or so ago. He's placing stacks of records of yet more grinning men with accordions into alphabetised hardboard browsers, and he looks at us with frightened eyes like a beef cow being driven into a killing tunnel at the local abattoir.

"Hello," I say to break the silence and the man finally meets our gaze.

"Yes?" he says, standing protectively in front of his display of records lest we sully them with our Beatnik sensibilities.

"Have you got Bread and Butter?" my sister asks, cutting straight to the chase.

"By the New Beats," I add in clarification before he sends us to the snack bar along the road. "You know, *I like bread and butter…*"

I know that my singing's not the best in the world but the man just looks at us in horrified silence and puffs out his chest like a cornered dormouse who's trying his hardest to look intimidating to a large tom cat.

"They're American," my sister says hopefully, "you know, on Radio Luxembourg…"

The little man finally shakes his head, mentally cursing the day he thought better of stretching barbed wire across his threshold. "No," he says gravely, "I don't stock anything like *that…*"

"Guess we're not buying it today, then," my sister says as the accordion player sounds a triumphant closing chord and we walk out of the door and into the bustling street. Giggling.

## 8 - Teddy Boys

My mother has invited some of her ex-India cronies round to the house on a weekday night to play mahjong, and gives my sister money to take me to the Gaumont and out of her way.

"There's ten shillings there," she says gruffly, handing over a note, "that'll be enough for your tickets and an ice cream."

"What about chips afterwards?" I ask, cheekily, expecting a short sharp rejection, but my mother appears to be in a beneficent mood and digs deeper in her purse to produce a florin.

"There, that's all I've got left," she says, flinging the money at us, "go on, get lost, you pair of bally vultures."

\*

The film is a double feature and doesn't finish until nearly ten o'clock, and I'm a bit bleary-eyed and sleepy when we finally turn out into the frosty night and head briskly up the Murraygate towards the City Square and our bus home.

It's a smoggy and freezing cold November night, and we can hear the dismal howls of fog horns on the river as we clatter up the empty street, our footfalls ringing out in the silence of the winter dark.

"Gosh, I'm frozen," I say, wrapping my scarf tightly around my neck and pulling my navy blue school cap as far down over my ear-tips as it will reach, "I'm glad that we got that money for chips."

My sister glances briefly at her watch. "It's almost quarter past ten," she says, quickening her pace, "we'll be lucky to catch them open by the time we get there."

"Oh," I say, disappointment audible in my tone although I'm trying not to show it.

"Tell you what," my sister says brightly, "there's a hot dog van at the City Square, we can go there and eat our food on the bus back, how does that sound?"

*

The tiny fast-food van sits in the shadows of the entrance to the now dark square, its greasy counter a glowing rectangle of canary yellow in the misty night. I can just make out the dim silhouettes of boys in leather jackets standing around its heat, and a gaggle of perfumed girls are at the counter ordering food and casting backward glances at the male figures in the fog.

"Alright, this is where all the roughs and toughs hang out," my sister whispers as we approach the aroma of food and the lamp-lit Edward Hopper tableau, "so don't speak and for heaven's sake don't *stare* at anybody. It's full of teddy boys tonight."

A lump forms in my throat at the mention of teddy boys, as I have a cowboy story book at home where all the Red Indians wear animal heads, and I visualise these youths as similar bear-like creatures who creep stealthily through the fog with their glinting shivs in their hands.

And we're walking into a den of them…

I hold my sister's hand tightly and keep my eyes firmly on the ground as the girls in front of us move away and we give our order to the man at the counter.

"Just the twa doggies, is it?" the hot dog man says convivially. "Real pea-souper tonight, Lass, is it no'. Now, is it to be onions on both your hot dogs and sauce as well? Oh, just sauce for you and nae mustard for the wee lad. Okey-dokey, coming right up."

There's a sharp hiss as he opens a bubbling tray of sausages and a cloud of steam rises up and momentarily envelopes him.

Oh no, I think, this is it, the teddy boys are bound to seize the opportunity and leap over the counter and knife the friendly vendor and steal all his money, but the haze of vapour quickly clears and all is still well.

Actually, none of this seems to be as bad as I've feared at all. We have been here for five minutes now and there have been no random acts of violence yet. And, though I haven't dared to turn around and look, I can hear the voices of the people behind us quite clearly. The boys are talking about football and the girls are giggling, and they all sound fairly ordinary, so I risk a quick swivel round to check out what's happening.

I'm still very afraid and don't want to be caught watching, so I spin right round in a complete circle, taking in all my surroundings as I go. But the teddy boys are just standing around eating hot dogs and not killing anyone, so I turn again and I stare, though I've been specifically told not to.

There are five teds, all boys about seventeen in tight jeans and leather jackets with the collars turned up against the cold of the night. Their hair is longish and slicked back, and one has a tattoo on his hand, but all they're doing is eating hot dogs and talking about last night's match.

Maybe they're not so bad after all.

And then one of them sees me staring and shouts, pointing his finger in my direction.

"Hey you, wee man," he yells, and my knees start to knock. Oh no, I'm for it now and my dad's gone back to India and is not here to save me.

"Hey, wee man," the ted shouts again, still pointing, "your hot dog's ready!"

My sister nudges me. "Come on, sleepy, you're needing your bed," she says kindly, gathering up our food, "hurry up now so we don't miss our bus."

*On holiday at Butlins*

## 9 - Rabbie Burns, Walt Disnae

I had always assumed that the guy with the rosy cheeks and big sideburns on my Great Aunt Barbara's tea caddy was Elvis, so it came as a big shock to me when, aged nine, I actually read the label and discovered that he was, in fact, Robert Burns.

"Who's Robert Burns?" I ask my dad's spinster cousin, Bunty, as she pours boiling water from the kettle into the big brown teapot.

"Robert Burns?" Bunty says incredulously, "do you mean to tell me that at your age you've never heard of Rabbie Burns? I can see yon school you went to out in India not knowing about him, but your teacher here should have told you all about our national bard by now."

Bunty works at the children's library where she spends her days coaching kids from aspirant estates like mine in the art of being Scottish. "Rabbie Burns is a very famous Scottish poet," she explains patiently, wriggling the knitted cosy over the worn earthenware of the scalding hot pot, "he helped to put our great nation onto the literary map."

"And was this before or after he became a bard?" I ask, now totally confused.

"I think it's time you went to your first Burns' Supper," Bunty says with a sigh, lifting the loaded tea tray.

*

It's a particularly vicious January night and hail like frozen buckshot is slashing vindictively at our faces as we sprint from the bus stop to the welcoming yellow lights of a church hall on the Cleppington Road. Bunty hands over two half-crowns for our admission, and a kindly old lady takes our wet coats and hats, pinning raffle tickets from a large book to the lapels.

"I'll keep the wee lad's coat right here next to the paraffin heater," she says, smiling, "that way he'll no' catch a chill when you go back out into that weather. Now get away ben the pair of you and find seats, Malcolm McKay's doing the immortal memory tonight and it's filling up fast."

I have no idea who either Malcolm McKay or an immortal memory are, but urge Bunty to hurry lest we miss something, and we scuttle into the hall and bag two wooden folding chairs at a long table spread with a starched white cloth and decorated with lengths of tartan ribbon. A large portrait of Burns, looking even more like Elvis, sans the sunglasses and jumpsuit that he would soon adopt, hangs on the wall behind the centre trestle, and little old ladies are busy putting out thimble-sized glasses of whisky at each place-setting.

"Will you imbibe, lass?" one says to Bunty, "No? No, I don't myself, not even to drink the bard's health. Never mind, I'll put some Irn Bru in a glass for you and the wee laddie, it looks the same and you can kiddie on that it's a nip when they have the toast. Clever, eh?"

"What's a nip, Bunty?" I ask when she's gone, "and why are we having toast for supper?"

"A nip is a wee glass of whisky," Bunty explains patiently, "and we're not having toast, we're going to drink one to Rabbie's health."

"To his health?" I say, perplexed, and not even trying to work out how we're going to drink toast, "I thought you said he was dead."

"It's a figure of speech, Lambie," Bunty laughs, patting my shoulder affectionately, "now wheesht a minute, I think they're getting ready to start."

I look over in the general direction of the centre table and, sure enough, a grey-haired minister is showing a very fat ginger-haired man and his wife to their seats, and, assured that they are settled, the good reverend turns to the room.

"Good evening, good evening, ladies and gentlemen, and welcome to our forty-second Burns' Supper. I'm very pleased to welcome our very esteemed guest, Malcolm McKay, who's going to deliver the immortal memory address, and also recite the address to the haggis. So without any further comment from me, please be up-standing as Angus pipes in the pudding, and, let me tell you, it's some beastie this year. Angus, when you're ready…"

All heads turn to the back of the hall where a wailing sound like a banshee with tonsillitis is emanating, and a florid-faced man in a kilt who is wrestling a tartan octopus marches into the auditorium followed by the lady who had served our drinks, proudly bearing a large brown sausage on a silver salver as if she's just given birth to it. The noise, within the confines of the small hall, is quite deafening, but all the old people around the tables – who would cheerfully dismiss the Rolling Stones as a fearful row – are clapping and cheering the piper and his accomplice as they lay their burden down before the fat man at the top table.

"Do you know what's going on?" Bunty asks and I shake my head. "They're piping in the haggis, it's a very old tradition," she explains.

"Oh," I say, none the wiser but happy to go along with everyone else in the room.

Fatty Arbuckle has levered his large posterior off his seat by now, and he strikes a dramatic pose in front of the haggis, holding his hand out in front of him in a suitably neo-classical stance reminiscent of Géricault's *Raft of Medusa*.

"Fair fa' your honest, sonsie face," he declaims in loud pulpit voice, "great chieftain o' the puddin-race…"

He pauses for effect and everybody claps. Now I am *really* confused. It seems that we are not only going to drink toast but have a pudding race as well? And why is this character speaking in a foreign language? I try to ask Bunty but she signals me to be quiet for now, so I lapse into a perplexed silence.

However, the fat man drones on and on in a mix of colloquial Russian with a liberal smattering of English words shot through, and just as I think it can't get any worse he picks up a razor-sharp knife from the table, its polished blade glinting wickedly in the lamplight, and plunges it straight into the belly of the haggis which deflates with a soft sigh of regret.

I'm all for calling the police, but everyone in the hall applauds loudly, and the fat man takes a strangely effeminate little bow like a ballerina acknowledging her encore, and then we all raise our glasses and shout, "To the bard," before downing our Irn Bru at a gulp.

*

I put my fork gingerly into the greyish-brown stuff on my plate and take a tentative nibble, but am relieved to discover that it actually tastes quite good. Emboldened I load up with 'chappit tatties' and mashed turnip and try another forkful, and, yes, it's actually really nice.

"What *is* haggis, Bunty?" I ask, shovelling down another generous helping of the fragrant savoury mixture.

Bunty laughs. "I'll tell you when you're twenty-one," she says with a mischievous glint in her eye, "just eat your dinner for now. There'll be clootie dumpling for pudding."

"With silver thruppenny bits?" I ask, still busy with the haggis.

"No, that's only at Christmas, and at home," Bunty says, smiling, "oh, look, they're starting the immortal memory address already."

People are still eating but the fat man has decided he wants to begin, and producing a great sheaf of notes he starts to talk, fitting in his lengthy speech, a rather caustic old lady beside us informs us, before the last bus home.

"I wasn't much of a one for the school," the fat man tells us all, "and I could not make head nor tail out of Shakespeare, but when I first encountered Robert Burns all suddenly became clear to me…"

I shake my head in disbelief. I had read the Lamb's Tales from Shakespeare that Bunty had given me for Christmas with ease. This bloke, Burns, on the other hand, was a completely different kettle of fish.

Maybe it helped if you spoke fluent Russian…

## 10 - Talking In the Scots

"Today, children," Miss Ogilvy announces in perfect English, "we are all going to learn a Scots poem."

We all look around us in mystification. In all our ten years on this earth we have been specifically forbidden from uttering all but the occasional word in Scots. Scots, we all knew, was a mode of expression permissible only when it was written down, to be read out aloud or for Oor Wullie to exclaim "Crivens!" or "Help ma bob!" in moments of unbridled passion. It was certainly not a vocabulary that *good* children ever employed.

We may have been Scottish, but we were the children of Harold Wilson's reinvented Labour government, the sons and daughters of scientists and managers at the new Timex and NCR factories. Our mail was franked "Dundee for Development" and we lived, not in the cosy grey-stone tenements of the Hilltown or the Wellgate, but in chilly white-harled semi-detached bungalows on new-build estates with manicured gardens where our dads drove to work in new Ford Anglias. We certainly didn't consort with dialect speakers.

However, Miss Ogilvy seems adamant. Toady is the day our national language comes out of the closet, albeit with the restrained confines of an old poem, and will run rampant on our unsullied tongues. We will learn a Scots poem if it kills us.

"Our first poem will be 'The Sair Fing-er'," Miss Ogilvy says, suddenly speaking in a strange accent, "then we'll move onto 'The Boy in the Train'." We look at each other, amazed. A poem about a sore finger! That seemed to smack of anarchy in a world where poetry usually consisted of limp Victorian verses about fairy folk plucking little stars for fans, an image that, may I say, failed miserably with a generation that had been spoon-fed the exploration of the galaxy and the Sputnik missions since birth.

Miss Ogilvy raps her pointer on the desk for attention. "Repeat after me, children," she commands, "The Sair Fing-er."

"The Sore Finger," we parrot back, like little Bertie Woosters.

"No, no, no," Miss Ogilvy says, undoing a decade's worth of elocution lessons in one sentence, "it's the *Sair Fing-er*..."

"The Sair Finger..." we say ever-so correctly. Miss Ogilvy shakes her head and decides to move on.

"Alright, the poem starts with a little boy going to his mother with a sore finger. This is what she says to him..."

We listen, eyes agog.

"You've hurt yer fing-er, pair wee man, yer pinke, dearie me," she recites in an alien tongue, "Say that after me, children."

"You've hurt your finger, poor wee man, you're pinkie, dearie me," we chant like Jimmy Spankie reading the Scottish News at six o'clock, feeling like we're slumming it, but Miss Ogilvy bangs the wooden pointer on her desk, sending up a mushroom cloud of chalk dust.

"No, no, no," she says in exasperation, "it's not 'finger', it's 'fing-er'. Say it like it's two words. Fing. Er. After me, fing-er!"

"Fing-er," we eventually chant as Miss Ogilvy's smiling face says, 'By George, they've got it!'

Miss Ogilvy is a great believer in learning things by heart. We know all our multiplication tables faultlessly, all the books of the Bible and all the countries of the British Commonwealth. And today we are adding the Scottish language to our parrot repertoire. We chant through The Sair Finger over and over again, flattening its cadence and its meter, memorising every full stop and pause, turning it into our robotic party piece for birthday celebrations and guising at Halloween.

But somehow, even at our tender age, the implicit message stands out very clearly. The party piece stays at the party, the quaintisms remain walled in by the boundaries of verse. Like the promises we all made about staying away from the main roads when we were presented with our first bicycles, we likewise subliminally reassure our parents that we know that this is a poem, a curiosity, and that we will never, ever, speak in the Scots in our everyday existence.

A joke's a joke but there *are* limits.

## 11 - Let's Loudly Sing

One of the beauties of itinerant school teachers is that they only see you for an hour each week and, therefore, don't know you as well as your regular class teacher who has you under her care six hours a day, five days a week. Miss Petrie and Miss Ogilvy, for example, may not *really* have eyes in the backs of their heads, but they know how all our minds work and can stop possible pranks well before they are even fully planned, let alone executed.

The visiting art teacher, however, with her colourful macramé waistcoats and long flowing locks, is more easily duped, but it is the good-natured and rather eccentric Miss Colquhoun, the music teacher, who is the most gullible by far. Creaky chair jokes which the disciplinarian Miss Ogilvy would quash with little more than a look never fail in Miss Colquhoun's weekly music lesson, and paper pellets and rubber bands always seem to abound when the good lady's back is turned.

Miss Colquhoun is a rather rangy woman in her middle years. Her hair is an unruly bird's nest in an era of pins and lacquer, and she favours ill-fitting slubby skirts and mismatched jumpers with large pieces of chunky cairngorm jewellery. It is whispered that she swims naked in the Tay each morning; plays the piano, violin and trombone; and leads us all in soaring ballads in a strong soprano voice that can be heard up and down the lengths of our old school's quiet corridors.

There is one thing that the amiable Miss Colquhoun will not be sidetracked on, however, and that is the bi-annual Dundee Schools Music Festival, and our beloved easy-going eccentric quickly vanishes to be replaced by a fire-breathing Hyde-ian doppelganger when it comes time to select our competition choir for this Olympian song marathon.

I am easily graded in this endeavour, however, since I have inherited my mother's complete and utter tone-deafness, and myself and another musically-challenged unfortunate called Ewan Cuthbert are quickly expelled from the choral ranks within the first day of auditions. For the rest of my contemporaries, however, it now becomes a long and arduous slog for the next six weeks leading up to the early heats, and, to make matters worse, this year's set piece is an indecipherable Caledonian lullaby called *Ba-la-loo Lambie* which has everyone's tongues suitably twisted in a matter of minutes.

Normally cheerfully tolerant of early mistakes, the newly transformed Miss Colquhoun smacks the desk top violently with a hefty pointer and yells, not 'raises her voice' but really *yells*, "No!" at the top of her powerful opera diva's voice. The class look at her in bewilderment, wondering who this shrill harpy who has eaten our easy-going teacher and worn her clothes can be, but do as they're asked and sing the song again and again and again until the teacher finally acknowledges the early stages of satisfaction.

"Alright, that'll do for today," Miss Colquhoun says grudgingly as the dinner bell rings, "take a copy of the sheet music home with you and get your mothers to play it on the piano. I want you all to practice for at least one hour every day."

We look at each other bemusedly, since we all live in poky semi-detached bungalows on the nearby estate, and nobody has a piano in their house let alone a mother who can play it. However, our teacher doesn't appear to notice our confusion and shouts:

"Alright now, children, form a line to go down to the dinner hall. And I want you all to sing the song again as we go."

We look at each other in horror, but our new teacher-creature is firmly at our backs and we shuffle off down the corridor singing "Sing ba-la-loo, lambie, sing ba-la-loo, my dear, does the wee lambie ken that his daddie's no' here," crimson under the gaze of the boys from the class above who stand grinning at the entrance of the dining hall as we march self-consciously through.

*

The first night of the festival finally dawns and I go along with my sister to cheer our team on. My friend, George Brice, has been identified as the source of the one discordant voice in the choir and has been given his marching orders, but as his name is already on the official ballot paper Miss Colquhoun capitulates and grudgingly allows him to appear, but he is given strict instructions that he can only mouth the words and not utter a single sound for the entirety of the performance.

The festival is held in the giant auditorium of the Caird Hall at the City Square, and the participants all sit on the choir steps of the massive stage facing the audience while they wait to perform. In later years I would be part of packed audiences in this arena cheering for Jethro Tull or Led Zeppelin, but tonight most of the seats are empty and the majority of the crowd are parents or elder sisters of the competitors.

Miss Colquhoun, resplendent this evening in a red jumper and turquoise check skirt, stands nervously by the piano with the other music teachers, most of whom look as though they'd rather be in the pub or home watching TV, and the judges slouch at their special table at the back of the hall where they sit peering at the pixie people on the stage.

However, the competition finally gets under way and the duty pianist takes his seat, but before a note can be sung the judges introduce an eleventh hour change and instruct all the teachers to conduct a class other than their own in the interests of impartiality (or perhaps sheer bloody-mindedness!)

Miss Colquhoun is up first with the choir from West March Primary who sing the lullaby sweetly and melodiously, responding well to her gentle hand movements and natural flow, and the audience applauds enthusiastically at the end of the song.

"Very good," the judges announce, nodding their heads and smiling, "next choir is Strathmartine Church Primary School, Mrs MacGregor to conduct."

This is my school's team and I give a quick thumbs-up from the audience to George Brice as our choir pick their way down the steep steps and form in rows at the front of the stage to await the conductor, who appears to be missing. The teachers are, likewise, looking about themselves, when there's a loud clatter from the audience and a very large lady fights her way out from the middle of a crowded row and clambers up the steps at the side of the stage.

It's an era when a size sixteen woman is considered plump by her competitors, but this woman is hippo-huge, and her Halloween-cake-like face is already beetroot and flushed from exertion as she takes her place in front of my class. I see Colin Findlay, the class bully, grin and say something to his sidekick, Johnny Doig, and the two of them smother a giggle as the pianist takes up the intro to the song.

At the side of the stage Miss Colquhoun slaps a thin hand to her forehead.

The song is a gentle lullaby and needs very little movement from its conductor, but before we have even reached the first chorus the big woman is flapping her arms about and whirling and swirling violently like a pachyderm ballerina from *Fantasia*. Colin Findlay is openly snickering by verse two, with Johnny Doig not far behind him, and by the final chorus the entire choir has tears running down their cheeks.

"Thank you, Strathmartine Church Primary," the judges say noncommittally as my classmates leave the stage, still giggling. "Next choir, St Columba Primary."

"Do you want to stay for the rest of it?" my sister asks flatly.

"Not a lot of point," I reply.

## 12 - Just Like a Dunkey Engine...

After I turned ten my mother decided that it was time that I joined the Boys' Brigade, so, like some American college graduate getting his draft papers for Vietnam, I duly reported for duty at the North Halls, a grim deconsecrated chapel sitting broodingly in no-man's-land by the local bus terminus.

Of course, at ten I was too young for the Boys' Brigade proper, but, like all respectable Presbyterian youth movements, the BB had its own apprentice section – a sort of Hitler Youth division, if you will – which in those days was known for some inexplicable reason as the Life Boys. Its official mission statement was, of course, the advancement of Christ's kingdom amongst boys, but in reality like most other organisations of its kind, it seemed to exist solely for the ritual humiliation of kids like me in as many different ways as possible.

First off there was the uniform. At the big kids' BB they wore pill box hats that made them look like a convention of bellhops when they were on parade, which was bad enough, but our lot had to endure rather jaunty little sailor caps that we wore defiantly with our navy blue school jumpers. (You *could* get a proper navy Life Boys jumper from the Co-op store down town, but it marked you as a complete twat and I literally begged my mother not to buy me one!) Additionally, to make sure that we didn't get swiped by rival battalions, we were all required to wear a triangle of scratchy felt fabric bearing our company number that safety-pinned onto our shoulders, plus a hefty brass badge shaped like a lifebelt that we were obliged to keep shining and polished at all times. It goes without saying that in our full regalia we looked like the Munchkin chorus of a Noel Coward review.

Anyway, I show up at the aforementioned Munster Hall on a gloomy night in October and follow a tumult of brawling boys into the bowels of the building where a heavy-set bloke with sagging jowls and a whisky complexion is standing on a podium surveying the mayhem.

"Excuse me, I'm new," I say.

The man looks at me in amazement as if a dog turd on the pavement has just reared its head and addressed him. "All hats and coats upstairs on the balcony, quickly," he barks, gesturing the general direction with his many chins.

"But I'm new," I say, thinking that they'll want me to fill out a form or issue me with a hat or something, but the fat man just continues to glower at me.

"I don't care how new you are, Laddie," he says slowly, "no caps or coats down in the main hall. Now move it, at the double."

An arm grabs me before I can make any reply, and I see my friend, George Brice, heading in the general direction of the balcony and dragging me behind him.

"So you've been sent too," he says glumly as we climb the stairs to a precarious balcony that is awash with discarded boys' overcoats and wellie boots, "my dad wasn't taking no for an answer any more so I thought I'd better come and get it over with. Come on, we'll hide up the back until one of them spots us. Don't say anything to them until one of them speaks to you directly."

We're back down on ground level by this time when there's suddenly a loud chord on the piano and I realise that the narrow podium now sports a line up of assorted adults in uniforms that look like a cross between a Red Square May Day parade and a traffic warden's convention.

A tall woman with an angular Eva Braun face appears to be in command and she steps to the forefront as boys scurry everywhere, forming themselves into dishevelled higgledy-piggledy lines. "Everyone in their teams," she calls sharply, clapping her hands for silence, "and any new boys down to the very front."

"Oh, this is going to be *bad*," George intones under his breath as we skulk up to the top of the hall under the gaze of every boy there. I can almost feel them mentally affixing hazing numbers to our backs.

The fat jowly man steps up behind the captain as we fall into place. "Team, atten-shun!" he yells, slamming his piggy heels together while the hall follows suit. "New boys, that means you too. Atten-shun!"

We quickly shove our feet together and inflate our chests like tailors' dummies, hoping against hope that we don't look like total idiots, but suspect that it is all in vain.

A bespectacled man at the piano strikes another chord and the woman in front points to a quivering boy beside me.

"First new boy, raise the flag," she commands. "Team, salute."

Everyone's hands shoot up to their foreheads as the pudding-faced pianist thumps out God Save the Queen and the unfortunate beside me goes hesitantly up to a flag pole with various ropes attached to it and pulls at one at random.

Nothing happens.

An audible snickering rises up from the assembled ranks, so the boy, blushing fiercely, now pulls the other rope, but the flag merely starts to descend, so he yanks at the first rope again in desperation, only to find that he now has total stasis. Mayhem is breaking loose, so the pianist, realising what's happening, quickly starts the national anthem again, while a young woman from the platform goes to the aid of the humiliated newbie and between the two of them they manage to raise the flaccid Union Jack to the top of the pole as the music grinds to a stop.

"Team, at ease," the first woman cries. "Welcome back, boys. Teams one to three, small hall for jumping horse training; teams four to six stay here for marching. All new boys, report to me at the double."

*

We each have our craniums measured for a hat and are given our shoulder number and badge, together with a letter to our parents requesting fifteen shillings for the privilege. One boy is wearing a grey jumper and is severely reprimanded for not being in navy, but other than that our first meeting with the camp commandants is quite amicable.

The rest of the evening is spent being trained for one of those mind-numbing action movies where people seem to run from point A to point B and then back again for no apparent reason, and we scamper up and down the small hall and jump over a gym horse – or at least some of us do, George and I tend to clamber over it in an undignified jumble of arms and legs – and then dash up and down the large hall bouncing rubber balls. When that's done we march up and down to the rhythm of the specky man's thudding piano playing, until at last it's time to stop and sing the Life Boy song, a mournful dirge about playing the game and doing what's right. Then finally, like waking from some surreal nightmare, we're back in the line-up we started in and some other unfortunate is charged with lowering the flag to the penultimate Liberace rendition of the national anthem.

The jowly man takes precedence at the front of the podium this time and addresses the flock. "Team dis... wait for it, Laddie. Team... Dismiss."

There is a rumble of feet like a herd of elephants as boys head for the balcony stairs to get their coats, the older ones shoving the younger to one side in their glee at being set free. There's a massive bottleneck at the stair door, but the seniors eventually ascend, and George pulls me quickly to one side.

"We *don't* want to be in their way when they come back down," he whispers urgently in my ear, "believe me, I've been to lots of these things before."

There's a rumble from the staircase as he speaks and we quickly flatten ourselves against the far wall as the biggest and meanest boys from the troop burst out again and kick aside any of the smaller stragglers waiting to ascend as they cascade towards freedom and the main exit.

"Told you," George whispers, "with any luck the worst they'll have done is stand on our coats."

*

And so it goes on for the next few months. We run. We jump. We run some more. George finally cracks and deserts to join the wolf cubs, trading in his sailor hat for a green and yellow cap, while I perfect the art of keeping a low profile and volunteer for any activity that doesn't involve physically jumping off moving vehicles at speed. I soon discover that it's impossible to get out of marching, but I do manage to circumvent being drafted for the five-a-side football tournament by willingly signing up for tubular bells, and bong my bit of steel pipe with a mallet when the patient lady who runs the group points to my note on her big chart.

I also manage to avoid the ritual humiliation of raising the flag in front to the whole company, since it always sticks, but at the end of my third month the hatchet-faced captain who runs the show asks me to stay behind when we break up for the evening.

"Stand to attention in front of the captain, Laddie," her ever-present adjunct, the red-faced jowly man, barks at me, "alright, at ease."

I move my feet the requisite ten inches apart like we've been taught and wait to hear what they have to say to me, sure that I'm being kicked out because I joined the party that ventured into the wasteland at the back of the hall to see the pin-up calendar in the builders' site hut next door.

"You've been here three months now and your attendance has been perfect," Eva Braun begins, "and your conduct is a credit to the company."

"It is?" I think to myself, "all I do is hide in corners."

"Therefore it's my great pleasure to present you with this…" she says, handing me a balled up piece of string.

I look up at her baffled and a momentary glimpse of the human beneath the uniform crosses her features. "It's a lanyard," she explains kindly, "we're promoting you to team leader."

"Oh," I say, wondering what I can have possibly done to offend God in my previous life to make him so hate me.

"Salute the captain, Laddie," Jowlface yells, a smirk slowly spreading across his florid features, "you're an officer now."

*

In the main being an officer isn't all that demanding, and consists mostly of making sure that everyone on my team coughs up their weekly tuppence collection money and that the cash deposited at the end of the night tallies up to the correct sum for the numbers of bodies on the roll call. On the downside, however, if an inspection is called I have to take the flak for any of my 'men' having a badge that isn't gleaming and reeking of fresh Brasso, but, worst of all, I'm obliged to consort with the other lanyard holders, a strange group of complete yahoos who actually enjoy the weekly fare on offer.

"I can't wait to go up to the senior section," Porto, a jug-eared policeman's son, confides to me earnestly as we stand surveying the hall before flag-raising.

"For the change of hats?" I say with a straight face.

"No, no," he says in all seriousness, "for the camping. Just imagine, living in a tent and being at the BB for a *whole* week with no school or going home."

"Imagine," I mutter dryly, my mind's eye seeing the full horror of being trapped under canvas with this lot, undiluted, for seven whole days.

"So, what's *your* team doing for the display?" Haggis, a particularly odious pudding-bowl-fringed fat boy, smirks into my ear, breaking my train of thought, "*my* lads are working on a human pyramid."

"Synchronised chess," I reply, leaving to join my team before they manage to work out what I've just said.

*

In a quiet moment later that night I ask one of the more approachable adults, a pleasant-faced girl who I thought of as a very grand lady, but who was probably only about nineteen, what the display is and what my part in it might be.

She looks at me like I'm a complete imbecile but explains patiently.

"We're putting on our annual display of marching and gymnastics for parents in three weeks time, plus every team is doing its own special item. Have you not been training your boys?"

"Oh, of course," I mutter, "I was just checking…"

*

"OK, what are we good at?" I ask my motley crew, who, to be honest, are nearly all as inept at any of this stuff as I am.

There is a resounding reply of silence.

"Oh, come on, there must be *something* we can do," I say in desperation, and they look at me pityingly.

"We could all be sick on the night," one suggests hopefully, but there's a synchronised shaking of the head.

"No, my dad's been looking forward to this for weeks. He *wants* to come and see me in this."

"Yeah, mine too."

"We're doomed," I say with a weary sigh.

\*

The night of the display finally comes round and we all polish our badges to a white heat to withstand the beady eye of some bigwig from BB headquarters who's coming to perform the inspection, then we shamble around the hall to music in a rough semblance of a military tattoo. The audience of proud dads all clap our march enthusiastically, however, then we run to take our seats and the night's programme of special skills unfolds.

First up is tubular bells, which I'm in, and we bing and bong our discordant way through a couple of Scottish ballads, occasionally even managing a loose approximation of the melody, and then there's a tableau of what being a Life Boy means by the seniors who are going up to the BB proper after the summer.

"And now the teams present their own display," the captain announces, and every dad in the room cranes his neck to see what little Jimmy has concocted to make him proud. We're called on at random, and there's lots of running about and jumping over things as each team performs its particular party piece. The dads all clap devotedly, even when Haggis' human pyramid comes crashing ignobly to the ground, and eventually the Captain calls out, "Team Five."

My hang-dog squad quickly exchange into-the-breach glances and then walk boldly up the front of the hall. There's a gym mat laid out at the ready and the jumping horse waits in the wings, but I instruct my crew to form a line.

"The purpose of the Boys' Brigade is the advancement of Christ's Kingdom among boys," I announce to the auditorium, looking directly at the minister who's on the podium with the dignitaries, "therefore Team Five presents the Books of the Bible. First, the Old Testament. Team…"

"Genesis, Exodus, Leviticus, Numbers," we chorus, "Joshua, Judges, Ruth, Samuel…" and so it goes until we finally reach Revelations and slink gratefully back to the ranks without so much as a body flip or somersault. The captain's face is an implacable mask, her adjunct's openly furious, but the minister applauds loudly and the rest of the hall quickly follows his example.

"Lucky break," Haggis hisses at me through tight lips as we pass his disgraced pyramideers.

"Low cunning" I reply to no-one in particular.

## 13 - Behind You!

The Aunties are great fans of variety shows and attend the musical theatre regularly, and I always look forward to an evening in their company when I know that we are all going to the Palace.

The sixties have not been kind to old music halls, however, their cash-strapped owners treating them as out-of-date white elephants rather than the pavilions of dreams that they were built to be, and Dundee's last poverty-stricken hippodrome is no exception. Its ornate 1893 proscenium has been boxed in with pale blue hardboard in a desperate bid to make it look more modern, but even the likes of the mega-popular Alexander Brothers are failing to put bums on the Palace's by-now shabby red velvet seats.

Nevertheless the Aunties take us to see Scottish stalwarts like Andy Stewart and Alec Finlay with an almost religious regularity, and the Palace's collection of Edwardian painted backdrops keep me entranced through even the most dire of Caledonian crooners. I'm not permitted lemonade at interval, of course, in case I need to visit the little boy's room during the performance, but one or other of the Aunties always shells out for ice cream, and, if my dad's spinster cousin, Bunty, is there, I'm even bought a programme. (Something my mother regards as a complete waste of money!)

However, the biggest thrill of the theatrical year is Christmas time and the Palace's annual pantomime, usually presented by the

Downfield Musical Society, a prestigious amateur company who permanently book the old theatre for the lucrative Yuletide season. Bunty has a gentleman friend in the chorus who always ensures our party gets good seats in the stalls, and I sit entranced watching Aladdin in his treasure cave or Jack ascend the beanstalk, seeing only the boy of my children's book illustrations rather than the stocky music teacher in saggy tights clutching grimly onto the barely-concealed ladder behind the teetering plastic foliage.

However, all is not well behind the scenes in Pantoland, and in 1966 the Downfield panto is actually bumped to November to make way for a touring production of the hit Glasgow Alhambra show, *A Wish for Jamie*, which is being given the coveted Christmas slot.

"It's a travesty, that's what it is," the Aunties complain, "our good pantomime pushed to one side like a piece of trash for yon Glasgow folk's bit of showy nonsense."

I have no idea what a travesty is, of course, but reckon anything that gets us two visits to the panto instead of one can't be that bad a thing, and my mother doesn't help matters by saying wistfully, "Oh, but it's got Charlie Sim[3] in it…"

The Aunties sniff, a tad hypocritically I might add, as they themselves are likewise much enamoured of the said Mister Sim,

---

[3] A Scottish comedian who became popular with housewives as crooner in TV shows like "The One O'clock Gang"

but they eventually agree to purchase tickets to both productions nevertheless.

"After all," they say grudgingly, "Christmas isn't Christmas without a pantomime at the Palace."

I couldn't agree more.

*

We have managed to secure tickets for the second house on Christmas Eve and I have been in a state of high excitement all day, hanging my stocking at the foot of my bed at two o'clock in the afternoon and moving it every quarter hour or so. My mother is in a less happy frame of mind, however, cooking and cleaning like a dervish in anticipation of the Aunties' visit on Christmas morning, and leaving no fleck of dust unmolested lest she incur their critical appraisal.

Eventually, though, seven o'clock rolls round and we strike out into the smoky night. It's bitingly cold and the whole town is glittering with frost, but the top o' the hill clock gleams a warm yellow as our bus trundles past on the way to town and the Palace's bustling foyer. The Aunties are already there and stocking up on King's Oddfellows when we arrive, and, since it's Christmas, Bunty treats me to the half-crown special embossed souvenir programme. There's a lot of folding of coats and straightening of hats, but eventually, like the waves of the Red Sea parting for Moses, our party surges forward into the auditorium and we take our seats.

The house is packed and I nestle in beside Bunty who's always good for Quality Street and augmenting the programme with her own knowledge of who's who and what's what, and we're busy scanning the cast biographies together when the lights suddenly go down and the orchestra launch into a spirited overture. Used to the modest budgets of the local company I am bowled over by the lavishness of this out-of-town production, with its layers of backcloths, moving projections and, best of all, a myriad of puppets to play the elf and kelpie parts as Jamie ventures down to the sinister kingdom of the frogs to reclaim his stolen voice.

It is, without a doubt, the most wonderful show I have ever seen in my life and prompts me to recreate it over and over again as a shoebox toy theatre all through January, but the Aunties are not so easily wooed by the Glasgow interlopers.

"My, what an awfy trauchle over nothing," the old ladies proclaim vexedly as we exit into the glittering night and join the queue at the crowded taxi rank, "and so noisy too, no nice tunes at all, and as for yon puppets, well, they were just a distraction, so they were."

I'm about to voice an opinion to the contrary when Bunty squeezes my hand warningly, and my mother's voice fills the momentary silence with a new stream of complaint.

"And where was Charlie Sim?" she laments, "the Courier said that he was going to be in this, but we never saw the blighter at all."

"Oh, away, he was there right through," one of the Aunties scolds, "were you sleeping through the performance, Rose?"

"Where?" my mother asks, hovering dangerously near the belligerent.

"You've not recognised him in his makeup, Rosie," Bunty intercedes, "he was the dame, one of the major roles."

"The dame? You mean that funny fellow in the frock? That was Charlie Sim? Speaking in that stupid voice? *That* was Charlie Sim? Oh my God, what a bally swizz, and he never even sang a proper song…"

"Aye, well, Max loved it," Bunty says, putting an arm round me, "didn't you, Lambie?"

I nod cautiously, aware that I'm being used as a pawn in the grown-up's dispute, when a soft and well-modulated Scottish voice interrupts.

"Hope you enjoyed the show, ladies," he says, "and I promise not to wear a frock the next time I'm in Dundee. Have a good time, now, and a Merry Christmas to you all." And then he vanishes into a waiting black car and is whisked off into the starry night.

"Oh my God," my mother whispers, "*that* was Charlie Sim…"

## 14 - Though the Carnival is Over...

It is around the time of my eleventh birthday that a curiosity about what the opposite sex keeps in its underwear begins to become apparent amongst myself and my friends. Even the taciturn George Brice, who wants to be a chef when he grows up and normally spends his free time thinking up new flavour combinations for fondant crèmes, suddenly becomes obsessed with female nudity and talks unceasingly about a boy in the year above us who allegedly possesses magazines on the subject stolen from his father in the merchant navy.

Whether or not these mythical publications actually exist or not is never put to the test, however, as the boy in question would rather attend piano lessons with his younger sisters than be seen consorting with boys of a junior year, but shrewd observation on my part determines that such items can, in fact, be purchased by people with the necessary finance and chutzpah.

All our families buy their papers from a tiny local emporium known as The Kiosk, a six foot wide by about four foot deep newsstand facing the meandering Gelly Burn that divides our aspirant new housing estate from the adjoining post-war council one, and this diminutive retailer is also our sole source of confectionery, ice lollies and comics. The proprietor, a wry manic depressive called Syd who has been known to compose impromptu operas on a whim, keeps all the local papers on his counter and an array of magazines hanging from pegs on the rear wall, and I have spotted, just behind his left ear, one or two garishly-coloured publications that feature bikini-clad young women on their covers.

I impart this observation to George, who nods glumly but rejects any suggestion for an attempted contraband purchase.

"We *can't* go and buy dirty books from the Kiosk," George says to me with the weary patience of an arch schemer who has already tortuously worked his way through all the ramifications of this particular course of action, "Syd knows all of us and, worse, he knows who our parents are and where we live. No, that plan's completely out. Anyway, these things cost five bob each, where are we going to get that kind of money?"

I scratch my head. "On instalments, like my mum's club book?" I muse aloud and George suddenly slaps me on the back.

"Genius!" he exclaims.

"I am?" I say. "Why?"

"Because that's how we'll do it. We'll get a group together and we'll all put in a shilling each, that way we'll get five bob no bother. And we can take turns at keeping the magazine."

"Oh," I say, "but how do we get round Syd?"

"We won't. We'll go to a shop where nobody knows us. Hmm,

we'd better make it one and three a share to cover bus fares..."

*

The potential flaw in our master plan, however, is that we are all eleven years old and technically too young to be sold girlie magazines, but George reckons that if they are requested as the sandwich filling between a typical dad's news order of the Sporting Post or the Tully[4] very few eyebrows will be raised. With this master plan in mind, then, we select a small but very busy newsagents at the Top of the Hill as our dealer of choice, and calculate the combined cost of the venture before going out to find investors to put the scheme into action.

Surprisingly, money flows quickly in and we are ready to make a purchase by the following weekend. George, as the brains and dashing double-oh behind the scheme, is elected to be the actual purchaser, while I am relegated to the more Moneypenny-like role of sidekick and trainer. However, after much debate it is decided that we should leave nothing to chance on the day, and George turns his reversible jerkin inside out and borrows a balaclava and a football scarf so that most of his face will be concealed. We also select a retailer who has an open-to-the-street front with a healthy pedestrian count on the sidewalk, and we time our raid to coincide with the exodus from Dens Park football ground on Saturday afternoon so that we can be immediately swallowed up by the crowd should things turn sour.

---

[4] The Dundee Evening Telegraph

Additionally, I've been watching some old Ealing prisoner-of-war film on television, and convince George that he also needs a watertight cover story in case he's questioned, and by the time D-Day comes round I have my eager pupil word perfect with his false name and address, plus the name of the callous father who has sent his little boy out to buy the racing results and pornography.

Half-past four eventually rolls round and we take the bus to the Hilltown and lie in wait by the clock till the men from the match start to flow along the pavements, watching them dotting into the chip shops or queuing patiently outside the pubs. We watch for another five minutes, then, when the pedestrian traffic is flowing thick and fast, George makes his move while I stand lookout at the other side of the street, ready to sound the secret signal in the event of danger.

The little shop is busy and there's already a queue of men buying tobacco and the evening sports paper ahead of him when he arrives, but our intrepid Steve McQueen finally reaches the counter.

"Sporting Post and Carnival, please," he says, his frightened eyes and nose peering just above the counter.

"Five and six, Love," the bored woman says, taking his money without looking at him, "next!"

And it is done. We stand gasping for breath around the corner, amazed at the ease with which we have fulfilled our mission, our hearts still beating like hammers as we prepare our debriefing for the group.

"I can't wait till we get home," George says to me when we have finally re-established normal breathing, "open it."

"Here?" I ask uncertainly, "I thought the plan was we took it back home first."

George looks about him. We are in a dingy side wynd behind a fish monger's that doesn't smell at all savoury and is unlikely to invite passing traffic.

"It'll be okay," he says breathlessly, a lump forming in his throat, "open it."

I slide the magazine gingerly out of the haversack we have brought for the purpose like an art thief unwrapping stolen Picassos, and George eagerly flips the pages. There are portraits of beauty queens in swim suits, saucy Arthur Ferrier cartoons of scantily clad lovelies, short stories about soldiers and secret agents, and, in garish Kodachrome in the centre pages, a large colour photograph of a chubby girl in a red & white checked shirt and shorts, her blouse blatantly unbuttoned and her bounteous breasts exposed.

"Easy on the Ahhs – Paula Paige!" the caption reads.

George looks at me and just about suppresses a giggle. "We did it, Max," he says with sheer naked incredulity in his voice, "we just went and blooming well did it."

I nod, suddenly aware of the huge cultural milestone that we have just passed.

Tonight we will no longer go to bed as mere boys.

We will be men…

# PART TWO

## DUNDEE, SCOTLAND
## 1970-75

*With my Aunty Violet and Uncle Ken,
London 1970*

## 15  - West End Theatricals

Britain is sweltering in a heat wave when we alight at Heathrow in the blazing July of 1970, but, having just spent three years in Pakistan, my family are still all wrapped up like Eskimos.

"There!  There they are!  They're the ones in the bloody stupid coats!" a voice yells, and I look across the crowded concourse to see a clone of my mother leaping up and down behind the customs barriers.

"Hello, Aunty Violet," I call out, waving, "how are you doing?"

"Max?  Oh my God, is that Max?  My God, what have they been bally feeding you, boy?  Baby Bio?  You were only up to my belly button when you left, what a damn size you've grown to.  Come and give me a kiss… *What?*  It's my nephew, he's not passing bally contraband to me, he's giving me a kiss.  Of course he hasn't got anything to declare, the boy's only fourteen, give him time, for God's sake."

I stand trying not to laugh as two burly men in uniform manhandle my mad aunt back from the customs barrier, then quickly go to join my parents at the "Nothing to Declare" gate, where my father is pushing our luggage on a skittering trolley with a wonky wheel.

"Come on, Slacker, lend a hand," my dad scolds, "I'm not pushing this thing all the way to London myself."

"Okay, no problem," I laugh, getting behind the loaded gurney, "but brace yourself, Violet's at the gate, if she hasn't been arrested."

Dad treats me to one of his famous snorts, which aptly sums up his opinion of my mother's elder sister.

"Rose! Rose! Chic! Over here!" Violet's voice yells as she literally jumps onto the trolley in her eagerness to hug everyone. "Where the hell have you all been, we've been waiting for hours and I'm dying for a cup of tea and a pee, but the buggers charge you for everything here, I though I was going to have to go in an empty bottle. Oh, look at him blush, it's alright, your old aunty's only pulling your leg. Oh my God, look at *these* blighters! *Hello boys!*"

A team of strapping African athletes headed for the Commonwealth Games in Edinburgh squeeze, grinning, by our bizarre tableau, accompanied by a rather staid reporter from the BBC who is trying unsuccessfully to record a quote for the evening's news.

"Hey, what about us," Violet calls to his back, "don't you want to interview my sister with your microphone? She's part of the Commonwealth too!"

"For God's sake, be quiet, woman," my Uncle Ken, an ulcerous man whose countenance wears a look of perpetual embarrassment, mutters in a subdued undertone as he shakes hands all round. "Hello, hello, all of you, have you had a good trip? I *told* Violet you were getting here at three-thirty but she insisted that it was half-past one, so we've been here for hours. Come on, don't bother with the taxi rank, they're all thieves. We'll see if we can get an off-the-meter mini-cab in the long-stay car park."

*

Our little party forms a perfect Norman Rockwell tableau over the next few days, competing aggressively for the title of Hicks in the City as we trail around a sweltering capital that's still basking in the afterglow of the swinging sixties. Violet and her husband rarely leave their secluded Welsh valley, reluctant to cross the tariff barriers of frugal living, while my own family walk around with eyes agog at all the rampant consumerism that surrounds them after three years in the outback.

I would like to say that I, too, am completely smitten by the sight of record stores laden down with every just-released album in the known universe, but, truth to tell, I am too completely bowled over by the sheer abundance of mini-skirted young women to even notice some of the material goodies on offer in the bustling metropolis.

"What's this damn thing, then?" Violet's strident voice cuts into my pulchritudinous reverie as we gaze on a slowly undulating lava lamp in Selfridges, "what the hell is *that* supposed to do?"

My mother walks around the glowing style icon suspiciously, sniffing like a dog. "I think it's meant to relax you," she concedes finally but Violet merely snorts.

"Relax you? Drive you bloody mad, more like. Hey you, what does this thing cost? Five guineas? You're pulling my leg, aren't you, boyo? You're not, you've never been more serious in you life? Bloody hell, son, I only want to buy a lamp, not shares in the damn store. Yes, thank you, that will be all."

*

Of course it's impossible to spend a few days in London without going to see a show, and we join the lengthy queue for tickets at the booth in Leicester Square, Violet quickly befriending some American tourists who are entranced by her accent.

"Of course you need to watch your bags, they're all damn thieves and pick-pockets here," she assures the gullible colonials, "and the women are all easy, I've already caught a couple of them giving my nephew the eye!"

"Not nearly enough of them," I think wryly, painfully aware of just how invisible I am in this huge city crammed with plenty.

We are nearing the ticket window by now and can see the array of brightly coloured posters promoting the various entertainments on offer, and, did we but know it, we're standing like kids in a sweetshop contemplating some of the most exciting new productions in musical theatre of the era, but neither family are the type to read reviews and so we simply stare at the placards, hoping for inspiration, instead.

"What's this *Jesus Christ, Superstar*?" my dad asks with a low chuckle, looking askance at a poster of a long-haired bearded man on a neon cross.

"I don't know, but it's probably some blasphemous rubbish," says my mother who hasn't seen the inside of a church for the last three years, "and I don't like the look of this *Pyjama Tops* thing either."

"Damn," I think, looking at the girlie poster, "that's a shame."

"How about this one, then," I say aloud, spotting a beautifully graphic piece of psychedelic art of a frizzy-locked boy and the single word, *Hair*.

"The tribal love rock musical," my dad reads from the small print, "what'll *that* be about?"

"Oh, it's a great show," the friendly Americans ahead of us chime in, "we're getting tickets."

"Can we go and see that, then?" I ask with hope in my voice.

My father snorts. "I suppose so," he says with no great

enthusiasm.

"Wait a minute, *Hair*, I've seen that on the TV," Violet suddenly says, having been uncharacteristically quiet for a whole sixty seconds. "Yes, I remember now, they all strip off and show their arses. What a hoot!"

We end up at the Black and White Minstrels.

## 16 - The Rink

"If you really want to meet girls," my new friend, Teeny, says to me back in Dundee, "you've *got* to come to the Ice Rink."

"But I can't skate," I reply, unconvinced, and Teeny looks at me piteously.

"That's the whole point of the exercise, ba' heid," he says very slowly, "if you can't skate then you'll need help, and lassies all like to lend a hand to folk in trouble. Just stand there looking like you're looking now and it won't be long before one of them comes over to help you across the ice and then you can hold their hand. It's foolproof."

We are an odd pairing, Teeny and me. At five foot eleven I am the tallest boy in second year, while at just under four foot ten he is the smallest, but it has to be admitted that he certainly has a way with the opposite sex that I'm anxious to emulate.

However, although I have never been to the rink, a shoddy down-at-heel hanger of a place on the Kingsway now long-since bulldozed to make way for a Tesco superstore, it really doesn't strike me as the kind of place to hook up with the opposite sex, and, still undecided, I intimate my misgivings to Teeny.

My friend looks at me witheringly. "Dinnae knock what you've not tried," he says with slow patience, "trust me, it'll be good. Now, make sure and keep some of your pocket money and we'll go on Saturday when the lassies are oot in full force. You'll cop a feel nae bother."

I need no further urging.

*

When we arrive at the rink there's a huge crowd of teenagers already circling the ice and crowding the surrounding bleachers, while a crackly PA system is blaring out George Harrison's "My Sweet Lord". And, as promised, there are girls, hundreds of them, but all with short jeans, butch haircuts and checked Ben Sherman shirts. They're certainly not the hippie goddesses I have been expecting.

"*These* are the girls we've come to meet?" I whisper pointedly to Teeny as a large-hipped blonde in white jeans and a tartan shirt pushes me roughly to one side, her gleaming platinum hair shorn right down to the wood.

"Oot the way, choob," she intones brusquely at me, her feet lethal in razor-sharp racing skates. "Oh, hiya, Teeny, gonna get us round the ice later on?"

"Sure, Doll," Teeny replies patting her ample rear, "pick a good song for us and I'll see you later."

I gasp, sure that he's just incurred the wrath of Isis, but, surprisingly, the girl, who's a good foot taller than him, doesn't clout him one but just simpers like an idiot instead and waddles off happily snapping bubble gum bubbles.

"Wow, can I do that too?" I ask in amazement.

"I wouldnae try it *just* yet," my friend advises, "come on, let's go get skates."

*

Teeny leads me to a hidden subterranean cavern far beneath the grandstand which, despite appearances, is not Hades, but the Kingdom of Eck.

"Number?" he snaps irritatedly from the gloom of his speakeasy flap, taking my five-pence skate hire ticket and looking me up and down suspiciously, sizing me up as the woman-chasing hound that I am with one sweep of his gimlet eye.

I look helplessly back at this taciturn pensioner in his jaggy flat cap and sagging braces, hoping against hope that Teeny will intervene and rescue me.

"Come on, Laddie, I havnae got all day. What's your number?" he barks.

I'm now completely bamboozled. "Number? Sorry?" I say, blinking like a fool under his steely gaze.

"Number seventy? Nah, nah, son, seventy'll never fit ye. Dinnae waste my time mucking aboot. Whit's your right *number*?"

At this point Teeny finally comes to my rescue. "He's not been here afore, Eck, he hasnae got a number," he says by way of explanation to the glowering pensioner, and, addressing me, adds quickly, "What shoe size are you?"

"Ten and a half," I tell the lord of the underworld thinking that progress has been made, but Eck just continues to glare.

"Oh, it's ten and a *half*, is it, posh boy? Well, *we* dinnae cater tae half sizes here," he intones dryly, "I'll give you a ten. Number fifty-three. Remember it for next time and dinnae waste my time again. Okey-dokey?"

As if by magic, or at least much-practiced sleight of hand, a pair of battered old skates that smell like something crawled into them and died appear in his fist, and he throws them in my general direction with a warning snort.

"Thanks, Eck!" I chirrup, thinking that now that I have a number I am one of the in-crowd, but Teeny jerks me quickly off in the general direction of the changing area and an aroma of ripe parmesan cheese.

"Just speak to him when he speaks to you," he says in the voice of one who knows, whilst seating himself and producing a wooden clothes peg with a hook in it and tugging at the laces on his skates, "here, do you want a shottie of my tightner?"

"No," I wince, making to get up, "these things are killing my feet already. I think I need to go and ask him for a bigger size."

Teeny looks at me as if I've just suggested assassinating the Pope. "You cannae dae *that*," he says in hushed tones, "Eck's already given you your number."

*

Teeny is gliding effortlessly round the ice hand in hand with the big blonde, exchanging sly kisses as they go, while I sit glumly on the splintery steps of the bleachers, the old wood sliced to pieces from years of skate blades tramping up and down from the ice to the seating area. The Tannoy is blaring the Middle of the Road hit, Tweedle Dum, which has a rousing chorus of "bum, bum, bum-bum-bum," but hundreds of shorn-headed girls are raucously singing it as "bum, bum, bum-tit-bum" complete with hand actions, and it seems like everybody is having a great time but me.

"Feet killing you?" says a voice and I turn to see a tall dark-haired girl, wearing a neat black Crombie coat over her obligatory check shirt and white Stay-Press, looking down at me.

"Just a bit," I say, looking into her big grey eyes and getting lost.

She nods, her black feathered hair gleaming like a raven's wing. "Skate hire, eh?"

"How can you tell?"

She glances at the number fifty-three writ large in white paint on the side of my skate. "The mark of the Eck," she laughs. "Just ask for a different number next time you come, he'll never notice."

"I don't know if there's going to be a next time," I say downheartedly.

"Oh, dinnae give up so soon," she encourages, actually touching me, "it'll come right for you if you give it time."

A ray of hope begins to glow inside me and I summon up all the courage that I possess. "I don't suppose that, maybe, you could, I mean, if you're not doing anything else, maybe, come round the ice with me?" I ask, blushing from ear to ear.

She smiles kindly and strokes my cheek. "Nah, I'm sixteen and you're only in second year," she says, shaking her head. "But thanks for asking us anyway."

## 17 - Bingo!

I lose my bingo virginity to my Aunty Violet at fifteen when my family drive down to the valleys to visit her this Easter. It is 1971 and Dad has just bought a new Austin 1100 which needs to be run in, and we decided that a jaunt to Wales will be the perfect journey to accomplish this ritual.

Violet is, of course, ecstatic. Not because she has visitors but because she has visitors *with a car*. Like my mother, she comes from a generation of British women who have never been taught to drive and is reliant on lifts and esoteric bus services, and my Uncle Ken is not a man who is easily winkled out of his armchair of an evening.

My dad, on the other hand, is putty in her hands...

A pair of inveterate gamblers, Violet and my mother have successfully reigned-in the family tendency to bankrupt entire households with a single bet on the gee-gees, but are each slaves to their own particular addictions nevertheless. For my mother it is the football pools and penny-slot machines, but for Violet it is most definitely bingo. In fact, if you could be such a thing as a bingo connoisseur then my Aunty Violet is it, and she knows every game in every hall, a regular pinball wizard of the smoky Welsh valleys, and a formidable contender for every jackpot going in her best headscarf and ancient tweed coat.

In my youthful arrogance I've dismissed bingo as a fairly simple game and so I sit down amicably enough to tick off numbers at the village social club, but Violet soon puts my misguided thinking to rights and leans forward to take over my card as the caller announces the first eyes-down.

We're all squeezed into various tables at the tiny club, me with Violet and a hoard of little women in headscarves, my parents behind us. "Three and nine, thirty nine, for four corners and a bull," the caller announces and the chorus of Defargians nod gleefully. This appears to be a good thing in their universe and the scritch-scratch of their pens quickly resembles the sound of knitting needles around the guillotine.

"There, tick that off," Violet, in her secret identity of All-Seeing-Eye Woman, whispers in my ear, "that's good, you only need two more to get a bull. Oh damn, some bugger's called it. Huh, Gwyneth Jones again, I'm sure her and that caller are having it off.'

Gwyneth's card is checked and the win verified. "All right, my lovelies," the caller says with a grin, "eyes down for a full house. Teddy's Den, number ten…"

And so it goes. The women all click and scribble away, snorting contemptuously when only offered a "line" but cackling like hags when something juicer is in the offing. Violet, in addition, also seems to have a whole storehouse of X-rated titbits about everyone who wins, and the endless night just goes on and on.

Finally, though, at around half-past ten, the caller announces a "Snowball" for the last house, underlining emphatically that there are only twenty-eight numbers available. "Alright, my lovelies," he smirks, "get your tickets in, only twenty pence a card and a hundred nicker snowball, what are you all waiting for? Also, the bar's closing shortly, so get those pints in, yes, you too, Albert Jones, time you bought a round, you mean old bugger…"

"Is there any food left?" Violet shouts, "I fancy something hot."

"Hot like me, love, like my leg?" the caller replies over the PA system.

"Some chance," my Aunt calls back, "I want something with a spring in it, not a leg of old mutton. Stick to Gwyneth, she's not fussy!"

The said Gwyneth looks daggers over at my aunt while I try to make myself as small as possible, but before bloodshed can ensue the caller shouts out, "All right, girls, eyes down for the Snowball…"

There's complete hush in the room for the first time that night, and even Violet holds her tongue as the numbers fall away, but no-one has a completed card by the twenty-eighth digit and the caller smiles commiseratingly. "Never mind, my lovelies, it rolls over to next week when it'll be a hundred and ten in twenty-seven numbers. What a win that's going to be. The lucky lady can take me to Barry Island for the weekend on that one. Satisfaction guaranteed, of course!"

"Yay, braggart!" Violet and her friends all shout, giving the caller the thumbs down.

"Don't say you weren't offered," he says with a grin, completely unruffled. "Alright, eyes down for the full house...".

*

During the week that follows Violet takes us on the Bingo Tour of Wales, to big towns and hamlets alike, hundreds of places with names that sound like throat infections, but all with one uniting factor. They have bingo. We go to down-at-heel miner's institutes and tight-lipped women's fellowships, quasi-derelict cinemas and flashy social clubs, all of them offering Violet's brain-numbing addiction.

And none of us win a thing.

But eventually it's the last night of our holiday and we're at some miner's social club in the middle of nowhere and things are getting desperate. The evening has started off with an altercation at the door as Violet's not technically a member and turning up with three guests in tow is considered a cheek by the two burly pitmen on the door.

"Listen, Violet Love, this is not on, neither it is. We turn a blind eye to you coming here 'cause you're a good sport and all that, but now you're bringing foreigners, bach, and that's not on, that's not," says the first, shaking his head.

"Dylan's right, that's really not on, Violet," echoes the second.

"Oh, come on, boys, have a heart," my aunt wheedles, "this is my sister and her family all the way from Scotland here, I'm trying to show them all a good time before they have to go back to their sackcloth and ashes. There's no clubs like this and definitely no bingo up there, in fact, it's worse than England, so it is. Don't be turning them away tonight of all nights, they're going back to all that tomorrow."

"They're never going to fall for this," I say, *sotto voce*, to my dad.

"Oh go on then, in you all go," the big doorman says resignedly.

\*

However, once we're inside the evening goes pretty much the same as all the others until the last house of the night. The ubiquitous Gwyneth Jones has already claimed the line – "How many callers is that bloody woman rogering?" Violet mutters – but the numbers on my card are suddenly falling away under the fat nib of my extra thick felt pen, and Violet, still in her secret identity, is becoming very agitated, jumping up and down in her seat and finally screaming, "House!" into my left ear.

I can't believe it. I've actually won, and after a whole week of pouring money into the coffers of bingo promoters throughout Wales I'm suddenly about to take some of it back home with me. I'm grinning like an idiot, pleased as Punch, when Violet whispers at me through gritted teeth.

"Stop smiling like a bally baboon and keep a low profile. They won't like this."

And, sure enough, there's a not-too-pleasant rumbling echoing across the crowded room, and I hear words like "interlopers" and "bloody foreigners" while my card is being checked. However, we sit tight and eventually it's confirmed, yes, I've won fourteen pounds – not a fortune but a lot of money in those days.

A few people clap politely and one person boos – only in fun, of course – but mostly there's just a moody silence.

"Keep your money deep in your pocket, they'll try to mug us when we leave," Violet mutters, and, for once, I don't think it's the family paranoia. My dad snorts and says I should give him my winnings as he paid for my ticket and Violet suddenly gets a funny gleam in her eye at the prospect of a share out.

"Nothing doing," I say through tight lips, "if we get out of here alive there's no-one seeing a penny of this. There a guitar back home that I want to buy before I'm too old to play it."

*With the guitar I bought from my Bingo winnings*

## 18 - Pirate Radio

"You have a lot of records, don't you?" Jeremy Taylor, class boffin and token English kid, says to me back home, a few weeks before the end of summer term.

"One or two," I say guardedly, not willing to admit that I have recently taken on a Saturday job stacking shelves in a supermarket to feed my music addiction. "Why?"

"Oh, I've started a pirate radio station and I need someone with music to run a show. I've only got classical records and I think we need someone who knows about pop, so I thought of you."

"You've started a radio station and you want *me* to be on it?" I say, rather cretinously, and my companion sighs exasperatedly.

"Yes, that's what I've just said, isn't it? Good Lord, how long does it take you people to get something? Come round to my house after six tonight and we'll try something out. Now, have you got that or should I repeat it another four times?"

\*

Jeremy's house turns out to be an old Victorian country manse that's been swallowed up by the encroaching city and a rather bland nineteen-sixties development, and I follow the sound of strident Beethoven to an old wash-house at the rear of the property. All seems deserted at first, but I spy some long wooden batons nailed to the gable wall and eventually find the said English émigré on the out-building roof fixing lengths of cable to his impromptu masts.

"Ah, there you are at last," he says without much warmth, "put those records down and come and give me a hand up here."

"What are you doing?" I ask, clambering up to the shaky roof, "besides nailing wire to a post, that is!"

"I'm glad you asked me that, Clive..." my new friend replies sarcastically, "but, seriously, I'm boosting our signal, the station's not getting out far enough yet. OK, pass me that yellow screwdriver on the left. No, not that one, the one on your left. Yes, that's it, your other left. That's great, okay, we're done up here, Beethoven is now being broadcast to the unwashed masses of Petrie Street."

"I should think that they can all hear it in their back gardens already," I say slithering back down to ground level. "Doesn't your old boy mind you making all this row?"

Jeremy smiles. "We have a mutually beneficial arrangement," he says opening the wash-house door and ushering me inside, "no noise in the house, no interference with what I do out here. Well this is it, come on in and survey the wonder that is our radio station. I think we can achieve great things from here."

"Hmmm, a regular land-locked Radio Caroline," I say noncommittally as I survey the mass of wires and cobbled-together electronic equipment, "so tell me again, how does all this work?"

"I haven't told you before, so I can't tell you again, but I'll explain it all from the top. I want to create my own pirate radio station that has music that people will listen to. After that we can start running adverts and make a fortune before we get to university. There, have I left anything out?"

"Just the bit about us ending up in jail," I say waspishly but Jeremy simply laughs.

"They'll have to catch us first," he says with a genuine grin, "now what records have you brought? Oh, good ho! Never heard of any of this lot, but if it brings in the crowds… But enough from me, you want to hear the station. Come on, I'll demonstrate."

I expect him to connect me to the blaring symphonia via headphones or something, but instead he picks up a little portable radio and motions me to follow him outside and into the street. "There," he says, switching it on and tuning to the station's very staticy classical music, "treat your ears to that. That's the sound of genuine illegal broadcasting, me lad."

"Puts Radio Luxembourg to shame, so it does," I agree, holding the little transistor to my ear, "but seriously, how far do those poles of yours manage to broadcast this?"

"That's just what we're about to find out," Jeremy replies, striding off down the street, "so far I've only managed to get to the end of the road, but I'm hoping to get to at least two or three streets away with this new equipment.  Come on, let's follow the signal."

"Maybe we should aim for getting rich by the time we graduate as a more realistic goal," I puff as I run to keep pace with him.

"Oh ye of little faith," he replies, holding the little radio up high to catch the broadcast.  "There.  What did I tell you, a whole two streets.  Now *that's* music radio!"

## 19 - Long-Haired Layabouts

The coolest kids in our year are a pair of disreputable schemers known as Kit-Kat and Toffo, and together they form an oasis of straggly hair in the desert of shaved heads and feather cuts that is my alma mater. Spurning the school uniform that my parents keep me forcibly clad in, they come to class in unbleached cotton shirts with velvet tank-tops and large floppy loon pants, and can be seen each recess blatantly smoking Embassy Regal in their own private corner of the school's unused bike sheds.

I am not, of course, privy to their exclusive circle, and it is only when Led Zeppelin announce that they will play the Caird Hall, and queues form outside Larg's the Music Seller's on the Friday night previous to the coveted tickets going on sale, that our paths happen to cross by a rather bizarre string of coincidences.

I have been unable to obtain a Zeppelin ticket since I have a Saturday job that prevents me from joining the overnight ticket queue, but Kit-Kat and Toffo have camped out and bought their full allocation of four tickets each and are planning to stand on the imposing Caird Hall steps and tout their surplus numbers on the night. However, when it is announced in the press that the hall management will be removing any would-be scalpers from the premises, a spanner falls into the works of their carefully thought out plan.

So, one grey winter morning when the sky is the colour of mouldy bread, Kit-Kat actually ordains to speak to me.

"Hey you, choob, you go to gigs, don't you?" he drawls as I shuffle past with a teetering stack of books for my O-grade English class. "Have you heard of Led Zepp?"

I do a quick double take to make sure that he's actually talking to me and then reply.

"Heard of them? I practically live with them," I say trying to sound cool and indifferent and failing miserably. "*Stairway to Heaven* is my national anthem. Why?"

"It's just that I have these tickets…"

"Yes, I'll buy one. How much?" I babble, totally throwing cool to the winds.

Kit-Kat pauses, and I can see the wheels turning in his devious little brain as he tries to calculate how far over the advertised price of two pounds I'll go to see my idols.

"Do you have the new album, Led Zepp Four?" I ask innocently, interrupting his thought process and trying to regain some ground.

"Naw, not yet," he replies, slightly disgruntled.

"Want a loan of it?"

"Shit, yeah," he says eagerly, forgetting momentarily to be cool and aloof. "And you can have the ticket for three quid if you want."

"Two-fifty and I'll bring the LP in at dinner time," I counter, jingling change in my pocket and watching him waver.

"Yeah, alright, okay, you got the money now?"

"Yes," I say, emptying my pocket, "here you are. Is this my ticket? Thanks. Okay, I'll bring the album along after dinner. See you then."

I turn to leave but sense that the King of Cool wants to say something else to me.

"Was there something you wanted?" I ask with feigned innocence.

"Er, yes..." he says, slightly hesitantly, "do you buy a lot of new LPs?"

"One or two," I reply cautiously, knowing what's coming.

Kit-Kat hesitates again then tosses his ash-blonde locks out of his eyes and abandons caution. "Some of us are going to the Grosvenor before the gig, come along if you want to," he says as though it's killing him.

I nod and leave without a word, trying not to jump for joy.

*

Our seats are seven rows from the front and dead level with Jimmy Page's massive stack of amplifiers, the noise so loud that it feels like being punched in the solar plexus every time our favourite guitarist hits a chord on his famed Gibson Doubleneck. The band play song after classic song, coming back for three glorious encores, and we tumble out afterwards into the smoggy night, ecstatic, our throats hoarse and our ears ringing like tenor bells.

The hall steps and the City Square itself, now that the concert is over and the management is no longer worried about illegal ticket sales, have turned into a regular contraband bazaar, and the whole place is alive with bootleggers and strange bearded carpet-baggers selling dodgy posters by lamplight, their worldly goods lying at their feet in battered canvas rucksacks. Kit-Kat and Toffo are practisedly indifferent, of course, but we all browse round the stalls and buy dip-dyed posters, anyway, taking them home to commemorate this stupendous occasion.

However, it's getting on for eleven o'clock and the last bus home by now, and I'm just about to call it a night when the taciturn Toffo announces, "Come on, let's go buy a joint."

My whole world spins around me. I have handled going to a pub, underage, without difficulty, and have been in my element rocking at the concert with the hip kids, but going to buy drugs is a different matter and probably too far out of my comfort zone to normally be tolerated.

Then Kit-Kat addresses me directly. "You coming, or are you too scared?"

"No, of course I'll come along," I say, reaching a split second decision, and Kit-Kat nods, cash registers dinging in his eyes.

"But I've spent all my money," I lie, "so I can't buy anything."

Their faces fall. "That's okay," Toffo says gruffly, sounding disappointed, "Manny won't mind."

*

Everything I know about drug dealers I've learned from films like *Shaft*, so I've absolutely no idea what to expect when we show up at the home of Manny Claire, Dundee's favourite supplier of narcotics to the student population.

I've been visualising someplace outlandish with a Cadillac parked in the drive, but it appears that the said Manny lives in a modest tenement flat in the Hawkhill, and we climb the dim gas-lit stairs towards the sound of muffled sitar rock that I recognise as the new album by Quintessence.

Breathless, we eventually reach the top floor and Toffo rings the bell – there doesn't appear to be a secret knock or anything – and the door opens flamboyantly seconds later to reveal a flabby guy in his late thirties dressed in an Indian-print tee shirt and scruffy patched loons. His hair, though shoulder length, is thinning badly on top, and rather than the cool hepcat I've been expecting he looks more like one of the two Ronnies dressed up as a pop star.

"Hello, hello, boys, come away in," he says in a hearty avuncular tone, "the night's full of brass monkeys screaming for a welder. Have you been to Led Zepp? Brilliant, eh? Do you want a wee cuppie tea? Diane'll fix you up if you're thirsty. Oh, posters, eh? From the gig? Anything good? I'm looking for the sixty-nine Hendrix tour poster, turn that up and you'll not find me ungenerous. Now, what can I get you lads?"

"Just a quarter ounce, Manny," Toffo says, taking the initiative, "for me and the Kit here."

"And what about this other one?" Manny asks, suddenly suspicious. "I've never seen this one with you before."

"Oh, he's okay," Kit-Kat says, "he just hasn't got any money tonight."

Manny nods. "Okey-dokey, boys, can't be too careful, the pigs have got eyes everywhere. Come on through but don't make a sound, or you'll wake the bairn."

Manny's hall is a myriad of psychedelic posters on red gloss walls, but he leads us into a dark room lit only by a tiny nightlight where the Hendrix hand bills are replaced by piles of soft toys, and, reaching under the pillow of tiny cherubic child asleep in her cot, he produces a small plastic bag from his modest stash.

"Piggy-proof hidey hole, eh," he says with his characteristic favourite-uncle wink, "mum's the word now, though! So there you go, quarter of Kathmandu finest, mix it with some Regal and it'll be so smooth you won't know what's hit you. That'll be four pounds, to you, thank you, come again, and you, quiet boy, get some cash next time. And don't forget to look out for that sixty-nine Hendrix."

*

It's well after midnight by now and the fog off the river is as thick as pitch, stroking our faces with cold fingers like a dead thing reanimated.

"What now?" I ask, ready for anything that the night might throw at me, but Kit-Kat and Toffo shuffle rather awkwardly.

"Well, we're going to our mate, Cosmo's, place but he doesn't really like strangers…" Kit-Kat says apologetically.

"So, we'll see you around," Toffo finishes for him, my usefulness to them clearly expired, and the two of them promptly vanish into the swirling fog.

I stand for a moment, breathing in the damp night air and listening to the mournful bale of foghorns on the dark river, and then allow myself a little sigh of regret. Like Cinderella after the ball my one night with the cool kids is over, and, I know, will never be repeated.

Plus I never see my Led Zeppelin album again...

## 20 - Sort Him Oot, George

It's a freezing night in the bitter November of 1973 as Dad and I get off the bus from Strathmartine at the City Square. Across the glittering flagstones the ten giant Doric columns of the Caird Hall face us stoically, a large and formidable structure which passes for the town's only entertainment complex, looking like it comes from Stalin's Moscow, its frowning Presbyterian architecture seeming to implicitly disapprove of every act it has hosted during its stern half century in the city.

My sister has screamed at the Beatles and the Dave Clark Five there; I have had my inner ear rattled by Led Zeppelin and Jethro Tull; and Yehudi Menuhin and Frank Sinatra alike have stood on its huge stage below the intimidating pipe organ and entertained a wide-eyed Dundee, but tonight we have come to see a much lesser-known but equally beloved artiste.

George Kidd.

Kidd is a local boy made good, a weedy specimen from a poor neighbourhood in the city who has overcome the limitations of his size and been the undefeated British Lightweight Wrestling champion for the last twenty years. He has a TV show on the local station, Grampian, and runs a couple of pubs, but it is the once-monthly gladiatorial tournament at the Caird Hall that really draws the crowds, and George is the star attraction.

Seating has been rearranged inside the vast auditorium to suit the evening's entertainment, the coveted ringside banks with their backs to the high stage with its polished wood choir steps and Phibesian pipe organ, the canvas square 'ring' in the centre of the floor. Dad and I are in our season ticket perch in the gallery, and we look down on a crowd that is in good form, chatting amiably like old comrades at a reunion. Programmes are rustled; plastic cups of strong tea wash down mutton pies ferried in from Wallace's in nearby Castle Street; and old women in their best coats talk animatedly together, miming killer holds and watching the ring keenly for the appearance of the MC who will start the evening's proceedings.

And they are not disappointed. The lights go down at seven-thirty sharp, this being no rock concert where the band can be fashionably late, and the promoters waste no time in getting the first bout of the evening into the ring. They're nobodies, of course, two very young, fit guys who have no charisma as yet, but who fly around the canvas at speed, bouncing off the ropes and showing their considerable muscles. Women whistle and shout out ribald remarks, this in a town where the female of the species cannot normally say "bloody" too loudly in public for fear of imminent excommunication.

Three rounds and a series of skilful moves later, a spectacular fall signals the end of hostilities and the winner's hand is held up high. "Look, you can see his balls through his trunks," a woman's voice cackles and there is more whistling as the red-faced victor darts quickly through the crowd and into the safety of the dressing rooms at the side of the vast stage. His trainer pats him on the shoulder, a get-used-to-it-son gesture, but nobody's looking by now.

The MC has announced the first big names of the evening. An earnest no-gimmicks guy is being put up as fodder for the camp antics of the fey Englishman, Adrian Street. The crowd boos loudly when they hear Street's name but he primps into the ring oblivious, looking more like the lead vocalist in a glam rock band than a villainous wrestling champion, with his long peroxide hair and gold lamé trunks. A man beside me mutters, "The poof's wearing make up," in disgust as the bell sounds and Street suddenly springs out of his corner and floors his opponent like a panther.

The crowd goes wild. "Pull his breeks off, let's see what he's got!" an old woman yells, while the rest of the hall unifies in a cry of outraged protest. The bout had hardly started, they complain, Street has taken an unfair advantage, but the referee allows the fall. One nil to the platinum blonde. The whole place boos vociferously but I cheer, this guy has got nerves of steel.

"Are you off your head?" my dad whispers, "you'll get us lynched doing something like that."

I say something really clever in reply, but it's drowned by the roar of the crowd as Street is flung to the canvas and the ref starts counting…

\*

There are more bouts and lots and lots of shouting, then a brief interval where people dash out for more food and a quick drink at the pub across the square before George Kidd, the main attraction. Kidd always plays Dundee. The town expects it, and the promoters always match this cheeky cheery local chappie with the baddest, meanest, cheating heavy-weight they can find. And this evening is no exception and the boos can be heard in Carnoustie as tonight's pot-bellied villain strides into the ring, masked and wrapped in a suitably Satanic red cloak as he scorns the abuse that is being heaped on his head by the dedicated Kidd crowd.

"And now, the mannie you've all been waiting for," the compère teases, "please welcome Dundee's own... George Kidd!"

There's a roar worthy of Hampden Park as the diminutive Kidd struts across the vast auditorium like a bantam cock, shaking hands as he goes. "Sort him oot, George," an old lady with her pinnie still round her waist under her good coat yells. George promises to oblige and leaps nimbly into the ring as the bell sounds.

The masked baddie decides to try Street's tactic and charges madly at the little Dundonian, who neatly sidesteps with a cheeky grin and sends his opponent careering into the ropes. The crowd roars, this is going to be a good bout. Dirty trick after dirty trick follows in quick succession, and the pinnie lady is up in the aisles from her very expensive ringside seat for almost the whole of the performance, but eventually after several near misses the impudent Kidd reigns victorious. As he always does, since, by some strange coincidence, wee George never seems to lose in his home arena.

"Gosh, that was *so* good," I tell Dad, exalted, as we walk briskly across the frosty square to catch the last bus home at the ungodly hour of ten-thirty. "I've never seen audience participation quite like it!"

Dad treats me to one of his famous snorts.

"This is sport, not your whispering Rep theatre, you know," he tells me with a straight face, "there's nothing made up here."

"Yes, Dad," I say patronisingly, "come on, let's get our bus, we'll just catch Mario's chipper before he shuts!"

Dad smiles. It will be at least another twenty years before I spot his sarcasm.

*My school uniform appears to inspire odd hand movements*

## 21 - Drama for One

It is a pitch-dark moonless night the following January, and there's a strong scent of mouldering leaves and smoky fires to the air as I crunch down the cinder path at the side of the unlit church and venture into the gloomy portico of the Small Hall. There isn't any sign of life, but the unlocked door yields to my tentative push and I look cautiously inside.

"Hello! Is this the drama group?" I call to the darkness and a voice answers me from the gloom.

"Aye, this is us, come away ben, we're on the stage..."

A chink of light appears at the far end of the room as heavy velvet drapes part slightly and a chubby woman beckons me towards her.

"Come up quickly," she scolds, "the hall's freezing and we're only allowed the one heater because of the strikes. That's it, in you come. Now, what can we do for *you* tonight, young Max?"

There are a couple of pendant lights burning on the stage and, as my eyes become accustomed to the dim glow, I make out a group of wooden folding chairs in a shambling semicircle around a two-bar electric fire and a group of portly middle-aged folk sitting with teacups and a massive tin of assorted biscuits that has been recently opened, the cellophane wrapper still on the floor beside it. I notice, absently, that they've already taken most of the chocolate ones and left the Digestives and Rich Teas untouched.

"Er… hello, I'm Max," I say by means of introduction, "I've come to join the drama group."

The group look at each other in stunned disbelief. "He's come to *join*," someone says, finally.

"And he's a *man*," another voice adds, "*halleluiah*, we'll get a play no bother."

Hands clasp mine gratefully like I'm the beneficent Führer visiting an impoverished Aryan gymnastics team and I'm deftly steered to a seat near the fire and handed the last chocolate biscuit from the proffered tin.

"Sit down, sit down," they say effusively, "it's *so* nice to see you. Will you take a wee cuppie tea?"

"No, thanks, I'm fine," I say rather uncertainly, "where do I audition? I've prepared some speeches."

The group laughs as one. "No need for any of that," a sharp-suited platinum blonde tells me reassuringly, "you're a man, that's good enough for us. Now, are you sure you don't want that cuppa? No, alright, then let's get on. Mrs Petrie, have you got The Catalogue?"

A very large woman who's still wearing her overcoat over her slightly-dated crimplene frock stands up quickly, brushing biscuit crumbs from her heavily painted lips. She smiles nervously at me as she bustles up to the centre of the stage, rummaging in her large Mrs Kruschev plastic handbag as she goes.

"Oh well, I'd thought we'd be reduced to putting on *No Time for Fig Leaves*, this year, that was for sure, what with only having Calum and Stanley, but now that Max has joined it gives us more leeway."

"Oh, don't keep us in suspense, Mrs Petrie," someone interrupts, "how many three-ems are there in The Catalogue?"

The large lady clears her throat and fumbles for her reading glasses, opening The Catalogue and running her finger down a table. "Three," she announces triumphantly and there's a collective sigh of ecstasy.

"*Three* plays to choose from, my, what a luxury," a lady beside me breathes giving my hand a squeeze. "You're a godsend to us all, Max."

"Er, what's that pamphlet she's reading from?" I ask, a little disconcerted by all this hand patting from complete strangers who all appear to know who I am.

"Pamphlet? Oh, you mean The Catalogue. We get one every year from Samuel French down in London. It lists all the plays that are available to amateurs this season."

"Wow, that's neat. And how do you select what you're going to put on? By the reviews or do you go by the playwright's reputation?"

"Oh you, you're a one," she laughs, punching me playfully, "no, by the numbers of males, of course. We're always so short of men here. Now wheesht while Mrs Petrie reads the titles out…"

The large woman with The Catalogue clears her throat nervously. "There's a thriller," she begins, but there's an immediate howl of dismay.

"Oh no, there's no point in doing thrillers with our audience. The bairns from the orphanage just giggle all through the show when you're trying to be dramatic. Are there no' any comedies?"

Mrs Petrie nods. "Aye, there's two. *Beneath the Wee Red Lums*…"

"Oh, yon's a hoot!"

"…and a braw new one about strikers. It's very topical what with all the power cuts and that, but it's maybe just a wee bit risqué for the kirk. Calum, you've read it, what do you think?"

A ruddy-faced ginger-haired man, who's been silent up till now, looks up.

"Aye, it's a bit near the knuckle, right enough," he says in a portentous voice similar to Andrew Cruickshank playing Doctor Cameron, "but I think the Session will pass it if we're discrete. But what worries me is that it's set in England and I'm not sure about doing all yon strange accents…"

"Oh away, we'll make it in Scotland," the blonde woman says, taking charge. "Are there parts for everybody? There are. Good. Then that's settled then. We'll do this one. Now, has somebody put the kettle on?"

*

Our chosen play, whilst not the Shaw or Ibsen classic that I've been hoping for, is a competent farcical comedy and a sort of modern day Lysistrata story where the wives of strikers down tools on the housework front until their men get their noses back to the grindstone. It has a couple of suggestive lines which are quickly excised, but the Kirk Session permits the scene where I take my trousers off and fall into a tin bath full of water to go ahead, thus ensuring most of my schoolmates show up to witness my theatrical debut.

The last three months of, often painful, rehearsals have been a stark induction into the ways of amateur dramatics for me, however, and I have quickly learned that tea break is the most important part of the evening; that no-one, *ever*, shows up for rehearsal on time; and that most of the cast feel that learning lines is for pussies because, after all, that's what the prompter is for. So it is no surprise, then, that the role of prompt person is the most demanding in the entire company.

There have been many, I am told, who have stepped up to this particular plate and been found wanting, thwarted by the cast's tendency to not actually *say* lines but just improvise near approximations of them and leave the unfortunate cue-giver thumbing desperately through the libretto in search of where the action is taking place. However, all this is now a thing of the past since the serene and unflappable Sally has joined the company, and she sits like a spot-lit madonna in the glow of her little anglepoise lamp patiently moving forward and backwards in her script as the dramatis personae shamble through the given text.

It goes without saying that I am completely in love with her, though she is more than twice my meager years and married to the ponderous Calum. However, I'm at an age where worshipping from afar is quite an acceptable mode of adoration, and I'm content to stand around with a suitably Bingo Little expression on my face and adulate her remotely.

Anyway, it's the first night of the show and I'm standing fretfully in the wings listening to the scrape of chairs on floorboards and sounds of an audience filling up the small hall to bursting point, the butterflies in my stomach doing an elaborate quadrille where they tie both themselves and my intestines up in knots. The drama society employ a retired makeup man who spent his working years cosmeticising for the huge stage of the Glasgow Empire and who applies the slap accordingly, thus making all the cast look like Red Indians on the tiny church stage, and I'm wondering if there'll be enough cold cream in the world to remove all this stuff at the end of the night when Sally comes past me with something on a plate.

"Want some?" she asks, pushing the dish under my nose, gorgeous even with a mouth full of food.

I look at the platter and my nostrils are immediately assailed with an aroma of fried lard that makes my tautly-wound stomach want to heave, but I stay as nonchalant as I can and ask, "What is it?"

Sally laughs and pops another grease-soaked morsel into her mouth. "Fried bread," she says, chewing, "I was making up the food for the dining table scene and I thought I'd use up the fat. Here, have a piece."

Every fiber of my being wants to refuse but Sally the Sex Goddess picks up an oozing crust and places it in my mouth, her ebony hair glinting like black diamonds in the reflected glow of the stage lamps, her full lips glossy from the fry-up.

I eat the fried bread as though I'm taking holy communion.

And it is disgusting. Alarm bells go off like clarions all over my body as my taste buds experience the joint sensations of lard and Leichner Number Three Stick on top of severe stage fright, and

I'm that sure I'm going to vomit all over the feet of the object of my affections at any moment.

"I think I need to go to the dressing room…" I start to say, clutching my mouth, when I feel a draft of cold air and hear the whir of the curtains as the main tabs open and the play-in music commences.

"Too late," Sally whispers, taking her place at the prompter's table, "break a leg!"

I don't answer but think that if I can get through tonight's performance with only this minor injury to contend with I will consider the evening a resounding success.

## 22 - The Last Waltz

George Brice approaches me about the annual Yuletide dance a month or so before our last Christmas at school and, before I know what's hit me, I find myself on a committee of two organising the festivities.

The dance is traditionally held in a rickety wooden structure on the beach at Broughty Ferry called the Chalet, but years of winter storms have taken their toll on the old road house's weather-beaten timbers and we find that it is closed for demolition when we make enquiries about booking the venue for our proposed shindig.
 The next best bet, however, is a down-at-heel ballroom in the centre of town called the Ritzy, and we ring the owners to ask if it's available on the night in question.

"Hold on and I'll check the book," the brisk receptionist says, flicking pages, "oh, the sixteenth of December, did you say, boys, oh no, that's after we close down for refurbishment, we'll not be able to fit you in. Oh now wait just a wee minute, Mister Geddes is speaking to me… Aye, that's right, sir, yes, they're wanting to have their school dance on the sixteenth. Oh right. Right. Yes, I'll tell them. Hello, are you still there? I've just spoken to Mister Geddes, the owner, and he says can you come in to the office to speak to him at half-past four the morn? You can? Oh good, we'll see you there, then. Cheerio the now."

\*

"This reminds me of the time we went out and bought a girlie mag when we were eleven," I say to George Brice as we sit in the anti-room of the busy promoter's office, incongruous in our school blazers, "only this time we don't have such a good cover story if he wants to know how much money we've got behind us."

"Relax, we'll be fine," George says with the unflappable confidence of the born entrepreneur, "the school's been holding dances every Christmas since it was built, he'll never question us."

"Yes, the *school* has," I say pointedly, "but this year the official dance is cancelled because of all the teachers' strikes, no-one's sanctioned the one we're planning."

George laughs. "Will you relax, Moneypenny," he says with a grin, "now wheesht a minute, I think I hear them coming through."

"Great, then there's still time to leave," I gulp, but at that moment two very large men in smart suits appear and block our exit.

"Are you the boys here about the school dance? This way, Mister Geddes will see you now."

I flash George a look of desperation but he's already risen to his feet and is following the two goons into the inner office.

*

Rod - the Bod - Geddes is a small stocky man in a shiny sixties' suit and bootlace tie, his long greying hair slicked back in a teddy boy quiff, his eyes invisible behind glinting silver-tinted glasses. He sits, smoking, behind a large desk that's littered with headshots for bands and performers of all shapes and sizes, and a smiling lady harpist lies cheek by jowl with a buxom stripper inches away from where I tentatively sit.

"So, lads," he says in a gravely smoker's voice, pausing momentarily to light another acrid-smelling cigarillo, "you're wanting to hold your school dance on the sixteenth, is that right? Well, as you know, the Ritzy will be closed by then to begin its transformation into Dundee's most sophisticated nightspot and be streets ahead of anything those bloody Chinks at the Hong Kong can dream up, but, never fear, the resident band are still under contract and I'm prepared to open up the old Locarno for your party. How does that sound to you?"

We both nod like car-back mascots, having no clue that anyplace called the Locarno even exists.

"It's a nice venue," he goes on, used to holding court, "I've had it in mothballs since nineteen sixty-nine, but it's clean and we'll heat it up for you. Now, I'll provide the band, the catering and the floor staff. You won't be needing a licence as it's a school thing, right? Okay, for that I take all the gate money for the first two hundred tickets at one pound each, and then half of every ticket sold after that. The hall holds six hundred easily, so there's plenty of profit to be made for your committee. Sounds good? Okey-dokey, sign here then, gentlemen…"

He proffers two neatly typed contracts, already monogrammed with his flourishing signature in somehow appropriate violet ink, and I look anxiously at the door in a last-ditch bid to escape. But his two 'assistants' stand silently at either side like wooden cigar store Indians and I realise that there is no turning back from this particular hair-brained scheme.

A large lump begins to form in my throat as I put pen to paper and commit to almost as much as my entire student grant for my forthcoming first year at university as I hear George Brice cheerfully say:

"Oh yes, Max is doing all our publicity, we're expecting a packed house…"

The rest is drowned out by the roaring sound of blood in my ears.

*

The freezing November gives way to an arctic frost-bitten December and the bitter industrial dispute between the government and our teachers worsens almost hourly, with each of the two education unions holding strikes on different days. Lessons become sporadic with large gaps during the academic schedule, and, as the pages fly off the calendar and Yuletide looms, most people just don't bother to show up for school at all, and ticket sales for our dance venture stay depressingly low.

Three days before the proposed fiasco we're sitting in the common room at school with a metal cashbox, tallying-up the sales over and over again in a desperate attempt to make the figures add up to what we want them to say.

"I *told* you this was I bad idea," I lament to the unflappable Brice, "we're at least fifty quid short of the basic gate amount, he's *not* going to be pleased."

"Will you relax," says George, sounding not unlike his mentor sans the vile cigarillos, "what's the worst he can do?"

"Oh, I don't know, send his goons round to break our legs, freeze our grants so that we're working for him right through our university careers, leave dead things in our beds at night…"

George Brice laughs. "You watch too many films," is all he says.

*

Although there are a whole two terms left of the academic year there's a certain finality to this dance, as though we're drawing a line on a chapter of our history, and we club together for a taxi and drive out into the sleety blizzard as if we're Russian revolutionaries heading out for our last night on earth.

We have sold exactly one hundred and eighty-one tickets, the last ten being foisted off on relatives of George's who have no idea what they've just purchased, and, despite the shortfall, Rod the Bod has given his consent for our final prom to go ahead.

The driver drops us at the unimposing doorway of the derelict-looking ballroom, its old sign dark and rusted, and we rush in through the sleet and wet to find ourselves transported through time to an era we never knew existed outside of the old films our mothers watch on television on Sunday afternoons. The shadowy walls are coated in faded velvet flock, and there are twinkling chandeliers and mirror balls everywhere, the polished parquet of the dance floor a shimmering cascade of reflected light.

Rod is standing by the door, flanked, as usual, by his customary heavies, his mirrored glasses glittering in the soft lamplight.

"Nice old place, isn't it, lads?" he says in his low cancerous tones, "I've a lot of fond memories in here, so it's nice to see it open again and filled with young people. Of course, I'd have liked to have seen it with a few *more* bodies inside, but, hell, it's Christmas, I'll let you off. Let's just say you owe me one. Now get away inside and have a good time."

We need no further urging and rush indoors, fresh-faced and eager in our best suits, long hair brushed and gleaming. The girls we have grown up with have been transformed into glittering young women in sophisticated ball gowns of gleaming taffeta and crushed velvet, and the band is playing a seductive song with a throaty brass lead.

Outside the snow is falling heavily against the boarded up windows of the old ballroom, but inside it feels as if this magical night will never end, and striding boldly up to the lush brunette I have never dared to speak to before, I beg the pleasure of the next dance...

*I think I was supposed to look irresistible to the opposite sex...*

## 23 - A Stranger in Blackie's Bar

"Give us two of the usual with a nip of motor oil for the Hunchback," Eckie Mitchie slurs over the darkly-stained Formica counter top, dropping a crumpled pound note into a puddle of stale beer, "but just a half of Guinness for Angus, he's got the van with him the night."

"What about Margot?" I ask, placing his drinks on the counter, "I can see the top of her wig in the wee room with the girls. Do you want me to get her something too?"

Eckie tuts under his breath and rifles his pocket for some loose change. "Aye, give her a double meths," he laughs, "tell her it's from her toy boy."

It is Friday night in Blackie's Bar and after only three scant weeks I'm just about ready to tackle my barman's 101 exam. Eckie Mitchie and the Hunchback are at their usual table by the gas fire, that's two pints of heavy and a shot of motor oil – rum and blackcurrant – for the Hunchback, whilst Arthur the Milkman (half of lager) is standing toasting his backside and delivering a highly erudite polemic on customers in posh houses who don't pay their dairy produce bills with suitable regularity.

Angus the Brickie, who's only on halfs of Guinness tonight because he's got the van, is in their orbit this evening since he's just been bought a drink, but he doesn't much care for the back corner boys.

Actually, he's only really hanging about in the snug bar because he's hoping for a call from a woman who wants her garden wall rebuilt, and he always gives the pub number as his business line. Angus is a trusted Blackie's regular who gets to put his drinks in the Tick Book, and, therefore, it's imperative that he's immediately connected when potential customers call, but he's also in the middle of a very messy affair with a visiting American widow so we all know that he's to be declared out of the building to anyone with a transatlantic accent.

A hand taps a glass on the counter and I swivel round to the optics rack and fill the empty receptacle with rum.

"Make it a double," a voice that sounds a little like a ventriloquist's dummy says brightly, "it's Friday night, after all."

"You're sure about that, Alfie?" I ask, my hand still on the glass, "remember last week."

Alfie scowls but hesitates, turning to his brother, Lexie, for confirmation.

Lexie gives me the nod. "Just this time, Max, then keep him on singles for the rest of the night. Let's try and keep the wee man out of jail *this* week."

Alfie laughs, downing his double. "I was never in jail, just cautioned," he smirks.

"Luckily for you," his elder brother admonishes, "since I had no money left in my pooch for bail by the time you were carted off, so you'd have been there till the Monday morning if they'd kept you in."

Lexie and Alfie are much-loved Blackie's regulars but are lucky if they make up the height of a normal human between them. Collectively known as the Three Midgets, the third member of the team being their little sister, Daisy, who's currently downing doubles in the wee room – a tiny broom cupboard with a side flap access to the bar counter – they are famous amongst Blackie's regulars for their acerbic wit and drunken cavortings. Lexie, it is written, can hold his liquor, but Alfie needs to be watched, whilst Daisy is usually quite safe if she sticks to Carlsberg, but becomes a man-eater when she switches to double Bell's with Eckie Mitchie's beehive-haired Margot. Which she is doing this evening.

"You'll be clearing the glasses in the wee room the night, Son," Tam the Bam, a practicing alcoholic and my fellow barkeep, says in an undertone, "I'm not fast enough on my feet to go anywhere near that place tonight."

"But it's okay for me to get eaten alive, is it?" I say, wiping the counter down with a cloth.

"Rule of seniority, Son," Tam says with, I hope, deadpan humour, "I'll still be pouring beer here when you're off at university swanning around in your cap and gown, so you can at least clean the tiger's cage for the summer."

I'm about to make some witty reply when there's a sudden hush across the bar and the outside door reverberates noisily on its squeaky swing hinges. If there had been a honky-tonk piano it would have stopped dead, and I fancy I can see sage brush blowing across the deserted pavement outside.

There's a stranger in Blackie's Bar.

*

As intruders go the stranger isn't terribly intimidating, a small weedy man with no hair and no teeth, bandy pipe-cleaner legs and a shabby suit that's seen better days.

"Here comes trouble," says Tam the Bam through tightly gritted molars.

"Him?" I say, trying not to laugh, "surely not."

"Just you wait," says Tam, vanishing down the trapdoor to the cellar and leaving me to deal with the stranger on my ownsome.

"What'll you have, Sir?" I ask as the little man looks me up and down like a dog who's convinced his master has a secret supply of biscuits in his back pocket.

"Is it really Bell's whisky that's in that bottle, Son?" he asks, still scrutinising me with his parrot-necked gaze. "Real genuine untampered with Bell's?"

"Absolutely one hundred percent, Sir," I lie, the liquid in question being about as true to the brand on the label as chips are to cheese, "filled it up myself only this morning."

Lexie and Alfie both snicker into their hands, but the stranger seems satisfied.

"Okay, give me a double and one of those strong lagers from the shelf there. And polish my glass, would you, Laddie. You never know who's handled something in a place like this."

I fill his shot glass for him and bend to retrieve one of the dusty imported lagers, a leftover from a whim on the part of another of Blackie's worthies, Mervin the Mumbler, who has currently moved to downing Glava liqueur mixed with vodka a good ten years before alcopop is invented.

"Visiting?" I ask, but the little man shakes his head.

"I'm a citizen of the world, Laddie," he says sarcastically, "every pub is my home."

"Till they throw you oot!" quips the tittering Alfie while his brother rolls his eyes heavenwards.

"Away and shut your pus, Tom Thumb," the stranger replies, instantly on the aggressive.

"Dinnae pay any attention to him, Mate," Lexie says diplomatically, though I can see he's not pleased by the slur cast on his brother's size, "he's had one or two already."

"I can see that," says the stranger, gulping down his strong lager, "I'm surprised that they let the two of you out of your padded cells at all, mind you. Do you have your own keys to the loony bin nowadays? Barman, another one of these."

"Naw, dinnae serve him," calls the Hunchback from his den in the corner, "we dinnae want his type here."

The stranger swivels. "What's that, Quasimodo?" he sneers, "have you no' got bells you could be ringing?"

"Right, that's it!" yells the Hunchback, jumping to his feet and spilling Eckie's pint all over the rickety table. "Outside. You. Me. Square go."

The stranger laughs without humour. "Away and dinnae embarrass yourself, wee man," he says tauntingly, "what are you going to do, join forces with the seven dwarfs here and report me to Snow White?"

The Hunchback makes a strangulated sound of rage and swings wildly at the stranger, who neatly sidesteps the blow and aims a swift kick to his shin, sending the enraged regular hopping across the bar floor.

"Alright, enough," I say, trying to restore order, "the pair of you, behave."

"Just having a quiet drink," the stranger says nastily.

"The hell he is," yells the Hunchback, still hopping on one foot, "throw him oot!"

At this point Kojak, the pub manager, a morose man who hates every drinker who's ever drunk in our hostelry with unequivocal loathing, appears on the scene.

"Is there a problem, *Sir*?" he says to the stranger.

"Aye, throw him oot, Jackie," the Hunchback and Eckie yell in unison, like an intoxicated Greek chorus, "kick the bastard right oot!"

"Perhaps you'd be happier in the lounge bar, Sir?" Kojak suggests diplomatically.

"No, I'm quite happy here," the stranger counters, "can I have another drink?"

I look at Kojak but he shakes his head imperceptibly.

"I saw that," the stranger yells, suddenly irate, "you're all against me. You and all your circus of freaks."

"Who are you calling a freak?" Alfie demands, sliding off his stool and confronting the Roman Agent.

"Oh, away and play with yourself, Gimp, I'm going," the stranger declares, heading for the door, when there's a resounding crash and a bottle smashes at his feet sending glass and foam everywhere.

"Just you leave my brother alone, you bastard," shrieks the diminutive Daisy, who has been on her way across the bar to the ladies room and fallen upon the fray. "Oh, not so brave now, are you, choob! Come on, what're you waiting for? Square go!"

"Daisy, *for God's sake*," Lexie begins, sliding off his stool to intervene, "just stay out of this and let the man…"

However, the word sticks in his throat as the stranger suddenly backhands him and sends him flying, his little body tumbling into the sawdust of the bar floor.

"You've hurt him!" Daisy yells, flying at the stranger, nails out like claws, while Kojak slaps his hand to his forehead.

"Throw him out," he says quietly to me and, leaving the fray, stalks out to the main bar again.

"What did I tell you," says Tam the Bam, appearing from the cellar trapdoor, "did I not just tell you?"

On the beach at Largs

## 24 - Final Curtain

I take to the golden light of western Scotland and the mellow red sandstone of Glasgow like the proverbial duck to water when I start my first year at University, and, clutching my newly issued student card in one hand I dive headfirst into the sumptuous world of theatre which is all around me, marvelling not only at the avant garde productions but the physical architecture of Glasgow's old Victorian hippodromes themselves, their gold-gilt prosceniums gleaming in reflected limelight, statues of the muses adorning niches throughout the ornate houses.

However, even with the generous discounts that my new student ID affords me, the never-ending parade of theatrical magic eventually makes inroads into the money I have so laboriously saved during my summer at Blackie's Bar, and come Christmas I'm desperately seeking some form of holiday employment to repair my damaged coffers.

I try without success to get hired as an ice cream seller at the Citizens Theatre for the panto season, but am unable to sell them on my usefulness to the company, but I successfully manage to schmooze my way into the employ of Scottish Opera and am issued with a bow tie and cream shirt and taken on as a temporary usher for their festive repertoire of *The Nutcracker* and *The Merry Widow*.

Thus, suitably attired, I turn up for my first night at the Theatre

Royal and am told by the stage doorman to report to the Front of House Manager - a slightly effete young Englishman called Clive - in the main office.

"And where's that?" I ask, somewhat naively, but the dour old door keeper merely shrugs.

"How should I know," he sniffs, "just keep heading up the stair till you get there. Someone will know where he hangs out, I certainly don't."

I thank him, not a little facetiously, and start to climb, the twisting stairway seemingly going on for ever, but eventually some ballet dancers in full Nutcracker costumes plus leg-warmers point me in the right direction and I stumble into the cupboard that masquerades as Clive's office.

"Sit down, sit down," he says, fussing with papers, "I'll be with you in just a moment. Now, remind me, who are you and why are you here? Ah yes, I remember, you're our Christmas man, come upon us like the stealthy December snow and gone by January. Alright, I'm assigning you to the stalls so I'm afraid I've got to send you down to the dreaded Mister Crosby in the foyer, you'll know him straightaway, he looks like something out of a down-at-heel Dickensian theme night. He'll be a total pain to work with, of course, but his bark's worse than his bite. Try not to antagonise him and you'll both get along swimmingly."

\*

Mister Crosby turns out to be a florid-faced old squady in full commissionaire's regalia, complete with top hat and epaulettes, and I find him strutting up and down the front foyer like an overweight bantam cock.

"At last," he yells in an irate parade-ground bellow, "six-thirty you're supposed to be here and ready to assist the clientele, not twenty to bloody seven."

"Sorry," I say, slightly out of breath but smiling, having just wandered, lost, up and down a labyrinth of corridors for what seems like the last hour, "I've been here for ages, I just couldn't seem to find my way down here. The Sugarplum Fairy finally showed me where to go."

There are about two solitary patrons milling about the foyer at this point, and my lateness doesn't seem to have caused either of them untold distress, but Mister Crosby appears to be incensed by my perceived levity.

"You couldn't find your way down here, *what*, Laddie?" he bellows, his flabby cheeks and bulbous nose turning from warm scarlet to flaming crimson.

"I couldn't find my way down here, Mister Crosby?" I try.

Crosby makes a funny spluttering noise. "The word you're looking for is *Sir*, Laddie," he says pointedly, "do you have *any* idea who I am?"

"You're Mister Crosby, aren't you?" I say, but my superior just turns purple, so I try, "Mister Crosby, the doorman," but this seems to only make him angrier.

"No, I am not the doorman, I'm the head commissionaire in this theatre, Boy," he yells, "I have twenty-seven staff who all answer to me and I'm responsible for the smooth running of every show this company puts on!"

I try in vain to get a word in edgeways to apologise, but further fireworks are postponed by the timely arrival of Clive who promptly banishes me off to the wilderness of third circle for my insubordination.

"I *told* you not to antagonise him," he whispers acidly as I leave, "you'll find the tips up there very meagre, very meagre indeed."

*

The third circle is a narrow, steeply raked strip of seating that hangs precariously from the rear of the theatre just below the ornate high-vaulted ceiling, and the stage can just be dimly made out far below.

The audience here consists mainly of impoverished opera buffs and students from the college of music, but despite the lack of tips at the bar there's a prevailing atmosphere of conviviality up amongst the high altitudes, and our little Alpine world is ruled by an incorrigible and very unoperatic redhead called Ina.

Ina hails from one of the large council estates on the outskirts of the city and works only at night when her mother can babysit her little girl for her. In an era where single-parenthood is as yet fairly unrecognised she is fiercely independent and survives without recourse to the welfare state, returning the favour, she feels, by declining to share her meagre income with the tax man. She has, of course, no interest in opera or ballet whatsoever and finds the sums of money paid out for tickets on the lower tiers obscene, but, when persuaded, can do a side-splitting impersonation of the company's current twenty-stone diva.

However, all the old ladies in the regular audience love her and knit booties for the baby, and can often be seen bending her ear at interval on the subtleties of Tchaikovsky and Lehár.

"The production is so fine, isn't it, Ina," I hear one old darling enthuse, "and the sets and costumes. Well, they just take my breath away."

"Oh aye, very nice," Ina agrees, having never gone near the auditorium after curtain-up in her life, "I liked the blue dress in particular."

"Oh yes, so did I," the lady gushes, "and she's so dainty on her feet, isn't she, just like a real china doll."

"You took the words right out of my mouth," Ina lies.

"Oh, Ina, you're so lucky, working here, I bet you just sit and watch the shows over and over again, don't you?"

Ina flutters her eyelashes. "Oh, you've caught me out," she admits and the old lady squeezes her hand.

"It's *so* nice to talk to someone who shares my love of the ballet. You're such a gem, Ina!"

"Oh aye, I am that," Ina replies without even the glimmer of a blush.

\*

December fades quickly into January and my time at the old opera house is almost over when Mr Crosby, suitably attired in his full uniform and gaudy top hat, announces a meeting of all front of house staff to plan for the up-and-coming Wagner marathon and the dastardly possibility of patrons blocking the fire exits with picnic baskets during the intervals.

"I need to get the bar set up and there's no point in me coming to this meeting, Mr Crosby," I start to say, I think, tactfully, heading for the stairs, "this is my last night and I'm back at uni tomorrow…"

Crosby's florid face turns an even deeper shade of crimson under his hat. "I've had just about enough of your insubordination, Laddie," he storms, "did I just say all front of house staff *except* one or did I say *all* front of house staff?"

"Well, all…" I begin.

"And are you not a member of the front of house staff at this theatre and under my employ and supervision?"

"Yes, but…"

"Then no buts, Laddie. When I say *all* the staff I mean *all* the staff, now fall in and pay attention."

I realise that there is little point in protest and quickly join the ranks of my grinning comrades as we prepare to humour our supervisor and listen to his pep talk. We're gathered in a neat row in the front foyer, our backs to the bank of locked street doors, when we become aware of a strange snickering sound just as Mr Cee begins to speak.

"Now listen up, this is important," announces our glorious leader, "the new Wagner opera is going to be very long and will have two forty minute intervals where people are permitted to bring their own picnic hampers. Therefore, it is essential that we be vigilant where fire exits are concerned and – what *is* that noise?"

The clamour beyond the glass doors now sounds like a hyena on laughing gas, and we all turn as one to the street outside where a hysterical drunk is teetering from foot to foot and pointing at Crosby in his outlandish outfit and guffawing uncontrollably.

"Oh, pay no attention to that idiot," Mr Crosby snaps grumpily, "now, as I was saying, the fire exits…"

"Do they pay you to dress like a prize buffoon, Jim," the drunk calls, tears running down his cheeks as he raps loudly on the glass to get Mr Cee's attention, "because I can tell you they're getting their money's worth!"

"Will you ignore him," says our boss, beginning to look flustered. "Now, the fire exits…"

"Oh my oh my," wheezes the drunk, "I've seen some prize eejits in my time but you take the biscuit, Jim!"

"Shall we throw him out, Mr Crosby?" an usher called Colin Mackenzie, who is Crosby's pet, shouts to his Number One over the din.

"How can we throw him out when he was never in in the first place, Mackenzie?" Crosby snaps. "Talk sense, Laddie."

"Maybe we should just bring the big shutters down?" somebody else suggests. "Or the safety curtain?" adds a facetious voice.

"*Quiet*, the lot of you," Crosby yells. "Ignore that fool and pay attention to me, this is important."

However, at that moment the doors-open bell jangles discordantly from the auditorium but my superior chooses to ignore it.

"Now, as I was saying, under no circumstances can people be permitted to picnic next to fire exits during the Wagner opera…" Mr Crosby bellows over the sound of the insistent bell and the cackling of the drunk when a new voice enters into the clamour.

"It's six thirty, Mr Cee," admonishes Clive the House Manager, striding briskly into the foyer and clapping his hands, "get those doors open, and you boys, stop dawdling around and get up to your floors, toot sweet!"

We all run to oblige, grins plastered to our faces, and, as I never return, Mr Crosby's plans for protecting the fire exits become a secret that he will take with him to his – undoubtedly premature – grave.

Orkney 1999

# EPILOGUE

## THE ORKNEY ISLANDS
## 1999

*My partner, Chancery, enjoying Orkney weather*

## 25 - Bondage Tape

"I think I'll be needing to make a wee trip to Inverness," the lady beside me says mischievously, "I'm almost oot of bondage tape."

I raise my eyebrows in what I hope is a suitably nonchalant manner and try not to look surprised. We are sitting at a harvest home supper on the Orkney island of Pomona, where the topics of conversation to date have been the poor crop of silage grass this summer and the favourite mallards in the following day's duck race. Bondage tape, if you'll excuse the agricultural pun, is something completely out of left field.

"So, what's bondage tape?" I ask, a little too casually, and she laughs.

"Oh it's special Sellotape stuff for tying folk up with," she says, tossing her blonde curls, her little blue eyes twinkling, "it disnae pull all the wee hairs oot of your arms and legs."

"Oh," I say, not sure where to take this conversation to.

"There's no place in Orkney that sells it," she goes on, oblivious, "you can buy it on the internet, of course, but there's a wee shop in Inverness keeps it, and she's really cheap."

"Is there a big demand in Inverness, then?" I say, a tad

sarcastically, but it's wasted on my short and chubby companion.

"Oh aye," she gushes, warming to her subject, "there's a big S&M club there, so the shop sells lots of good stuff."

"Oh, like what?" I say, intrigued in spite of myself.

"Well, I got my dungeon hooks there, they're a life saver…"

"Dungeon hooks?" I say, quizzically.

"They're hooks that go over a door to fix handcuffs and chains to. They're specially made so that they'll no' damage your paintwork."

"Very practical," I nod.

"Oh aye," she says with a wink, "there's lots of stuff you can do. Maybe you'd like to come over and tie me up some Saturday afternoon?"

I make a polite noise. "Maybe I can take a rain check on that one?"

She laughs and gives me a sidelong glance. "It'll just have to be oor peedie secret till then," she whispers, "now, which duck do you think I should put my money on the morn?"

# the last burrah sahibs

A warm and witty look at the unofficial last years of British Colonial Life as seen through the eyes of a small boy growing up out East in the dissolving remnants of the British Raj.

After being compulsorily retired from an Indian jute mill and returning to Dundee in the mid 1960s, Max Scratchmann's family cannot settle down to life in Scotland. So, when the chance of a three-year contract in East Pakistan (now Bangladesh) is offered, they promptly fly off to live the colonial life one last time.

Aided and abetted by the mischievous Mafzal, his paan-addicted driver, eleven-year-old Max rediscovers the forgotten lifestyle of his early childhood, and meets a cast of colourfully eccentric characters amongst both the émigré British and the indigenous population along the way.

On the surface, life for jute wallahs' children may seem to be an endless parade of swimming pool parties and badly-dubbed Italian art movies, but growing political unrest and brushes with street rioting show that these are indeed stolen years, and **The Last Burrah Sahibs** is an engaging and heartfelt chronicle of growing up in a culture that is now well and truly lost.

"Scratchmann tells his story and introduces his characters with the easy style of a practiced humorist"
**The Scots Magazine**

UK £8.50
ISBN 978-1-904246-38-1

# *CHUCKING IT ALL*

**N**amed one of the twelve best travel books of 2009 by Worldhum, **Chucking It All** exposes the gritty reality behind all those twee bestsellers which extol the joys of sunny rural idylls.

With its remorseless true-life account of downshifting to a remote Scottish island, **Chucking It All** uncovers the frightening realities of relocating to "a magical island lost in the mists of time" as you follow the warts-and-all adventures of urban misanthrope, Max Scratchmann, as he valiantly tries to forge a new life in the windswept Orkney islands, and grumbles his way through unending winters with eighteen-hour nights, nocturnal visits from drunken farmers and booty calls from desperate divorcees.

From struggling to fit in as a temporary postman in a wilderness where houses don't display numbers or names, to attending drunken country ceilidhs with the island singles' club, or finding himself up to the neck in local politics while performing in the village pantomime, **Chucking It All** is an urbanite's nightmare and one of the most hilarious books that you will read this year.

Irreverent, sarcastic and bitingly caustic, **Chucking It All** still manages to be a grudgingly affectionate portrait of rural life through the eyes of a cynical outsider, and is one of the truest accounts of "living the dream" ever published.

"Does for downshifting what Lewinsky did for Clinton – only much funnier..."

UK £12.99
ISBN 978-09571920-2-7

# How to Write the Perfect Novel

There are hundreds of conventional writers' guides on the market, but none so scathing, cynical and downright cantankerous as this one. Forget toadying to publishers or obsessing over return postage - in this insider exposé veteran author, Chancery Stone, spares no-one's blushes as she strips the book world bare and reveals the true natures of publishers and authors alike.

Interspersed with laugh-out-loud parodies of best-selling thrillers, romances, crime, science fiction, erotica and even the Booker Prize, and naming names and showing no mercy to the perpetrators, **How to Write the Perfect Novel** will submerge you in such brain-numbing brilliance that you may never browse through a book shop in quite the same way again....

""The perfect antidote to the thousands of well-meaning, hefty writers' guides that currently flood the market"
**Essential Writers**

"A bitter look at how to succeed"
**Writers' Forum**

"This is the kind of book that you read for the humour, the scathing remarks and the blatant flaunting of all the rules. Yet it is so cleverly written that you find yourself learning things that, quite frankly, none of the other how-to books teach you"
**W H Smith**

UK £9.99
ISBN 978-0954611576

## My Rubber Hebrew Nose

Max Scratchmann
e-book & paperback
UK £5.99 ISBN 978-1477635308

Meet the Pobble who has all his toes, share the Fish Supper of J Alfred Prufrock and discover the lost manuscript of a poem penned by Edgar Allen Poe on his visit to the Raven Hotel, Blackpool.

**My Rubber Hebrew Nose** is a hilariously insane collection of literary parody and nonsense verse in the great tradition of Edward Lear and Lewis Carroll, written and superbly illustrated by British humorist, Max Scratchmann,

Come and join some literary greats and their sexually deviant maiden aunts, as well as a stellar supporting cast of horrible children and errant vicars, proving, if proof were ever needed, that British comic verse is truly for life and not just for Christmas.

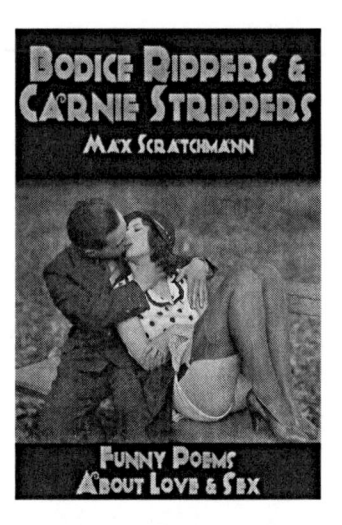

## Bodice Rippers & Carnie Strippers

Max Scratchmann
e-book only
UK £1.95  ASIN B00513D8DC

**Bodice Rippers & Carnie Strippers** is an eccentric collection of miscellaneous and very funny poems about love and sex, an unruly and anarchic anthology of deviant doggerel, which frequently mutates into breathy love poems, lascivious limericks and terrible tales of out-and-out shameful shenanigans.

Meet a hilarious selection of vapid vampires and hardened harlots, voluptuous Lolitas and their grasping grannies; as well as a suitably epic supporting cast of adulterous vicars, lascivious lesbians and nubile nuns.

Read it as a guilty pleasure or gift it to a friend with a wicked sense of humour.

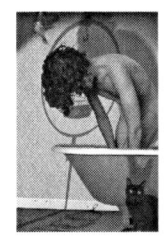

# The DANNY Quadrilogy

Chancery Stone
e-book & paperback

**The brutal and violent love story of flame-haired Daniel Jackson Moore and his obsessive brother, John. "A sexually-explicit modern-day *Wuthering Heights*..."**

**THE DANNY QUADRILOGY** is a huge stylistic achievement, a Jacobean drama on an epic scale, reaching into realms far darker than anything ever dreamt of in Shakespeare's philosophy. It belongs more firmly in the shadowy corridors of John Ford, the secret rooms of Christopher Marlowe, the feral imagination of John Webster - in short, in a place where gouging out eyes with steel spikes and unwittingly fucking your sister are commonplace tragedies.

For modern audiences, however, it may be imagined more easily as film noir, a long running soap opera from the dark side, something that HBO might commission as a creative pièce de résistance designed to out-swear *Deadwood*, out-abuse *OZ* and out-rape *Rome*.

It is the home of supernaturally compelling characters, blessed with the phallocentric charisma of sexed-up animals, goats in human form, satyrs. And they act out every sick fantasy in graphic detail, strutting their sex, violence, perversion and addiction as if they were proud of it.

It is beyond good and evil, it is simply necessary.

**"...a wonderful, unnerving, compelling and haunting collection of books of blood..."**

www.poisonpixie.com
Join our mailing list for free stories and offers